Marisa Peer studied hypnotherapy at the Hypnotism Training Institute of Los Angeles, known as the best hypnotherapy training establishment in the world. She has spent over thirty years working with an extensive client list including royalty, rock stars, actors, CEOs and Olympic athletes. Marisa has developed her own unique style, which is frequently referred to as life-changing.

Marisa works extensively on television and radio, appearing on Supersize vs Superskinny and Celebrity Fit Club in the UK and US. In May 2006, Marisa was named Best British Therapist by Men's Health magazine and featured in Tatler's Guide to Britain's 250 Best Doctors. She gives lectures and workshops all over the world.

To find out more information on Marisa visit:

www.marisapeer.com
www.rapidtransformationaltherapy.com

Connect with Marisa Peer on Facebook, Twitter, Instagram, YouTube, Vimeo, LinkedIn

. . . .

I Am Enough: An Eight-Part Program to Master Your Beliefs and Set You Up for Phenomenal Success

Marisa Peer has created a complete and concise transformational program for *I Am Enough*. Delivered in eight modules over eight video and audio tracks, the program will give you the same reality-shifting, epiphanic effects experienced in person by her high-profile clients.

It is designed to radically and permanently alter the key areas that impact your life. This includes your confidence levels, your purpose, your relationships, your career, creating wealth and abundance and enjoying a phenomenal sex life. *I Am Enough* is a brand new, cutting edge, exciting program that can change and redefine your life. After using this program, you can activate the abundance and potential that you desire.

For further information visit:

www.iamenough.com/resources

Previous Titles

You Can Be Thin: The Ultimate Program to End Dieting Forever

'I'm always skeptical at the thought of another "miracle diet" book but this really is different … constructive thoughts from a woman who really does know.'
You Magazine

'I would recommend this book to my patients or anyone who wishes to change their weight and find a healthy relationship with food.'
Dr Chris Steele, GP and resident doctor on This Morning

. . . .

You Can Be Younger: Use the Power of your Mind to Look and Feel 10 Years Younger in 10 Simple Steps

'I cannot recommend Marisa Peer, her methods or this book highly enough. You Can Be Younger is a wonder, a life-changer and a life-saver.'
Molly Parkin, artist, writer and celebrity

. . . .

Trying To Get Pregnant (and Succeeding)

'I am so glad that Marisa's book contains her unique techniques so that even more women can benefit from them…. I wholeheartedly recommend this book to any women struggling with infertility.'
College Murphy, Sands (Stillbirth and Neonatal Death Charity)

'I read Trying To Get Pregnant (and Succeeding) and it gave me wisdom, insight and faith during many difficulties and obstacles.

I am so glad I turned to Marisa as I now have a beautiful, amazing, wonderful son. Thank you Marisa.'
Daniella Neumann, TV Producer

. . . .

Ultimate Confidence: The Secrets to Feeling Great About Yourself Every Day

'People always assume that television personalities are brimming with self-confidence, but the truth is that we all have areas of our lives where we wish we could do better. Marisa's approach is effective, refreshingly different and, more importantly, enjoyable'
Anna Richardson, TV presenter

For further information on Marisa Peer's books please visit:

www.marisapeer.com/books

Praise for *I Am Enough*

'I don't know how to thank you! I've fallen in love with you, you really changed my life. The great thing about you is that you really say the truth, the truth that almost all other therapists do not say. I'm a lecturer teaching at Universities and now I teach my students *I Am Enough* and also make them realize their greatness. You see, being an instructor and standing in front of young people makes you see the truth and pain in them caused by their beliefs which they picked up during their childhood. So now I always have to tell them about what I learnt from you and the students would come to me so that I can write on their hands, *I Am Enough*. Thank you again, really, from the bottom of my heart and since I have got the chance to listen to you and learn from you, I no longer listen to or visit life coaches or psychologists.'

Shereen

'A few weeks ago I spent some time with my dear friend and one of the best hypnotherapists in the world - Marisa Peer. She will always have a special place in my heart because she helped my wife so much when we were struggling to have a baby. She helped many people, including celebrities and British royalty, to overcome their phobias, infertility problems, addictions and weight problems. A few years ago she started a movement called *I Am Enough*. It is AMAZING! She teaches people that they are good enough to do anything they want. It's incredibly powerful and she managed to help millions of people.'

Smiljan

'I came across a video on YouTube and signed up for the *I Am Enough* program. Today I am into day 7. I have downloaded the recordings and listen to it every night before going to bed. The effect is amazing. I used to be a very angry person, I am always unhappy and grumpy, especially at work. I fear every day... fear of making mistakes... Will I get scoldings today? Did I miss out anything important? The more I fear, the more mistakes I made! I always start my day with fear and end it with anger. After listening to your recordings, I'm surprised that I am more relaxed on the way to work... I am not angry, more positive and not depressed... the feelings just go away.... I was more cheerful and confident at work last week. My husband is the first person to notice the changes. I have written and printed "*I Am Enough*" and pasted it on the walls at my house and engraved the words onto my bracelet. And every morning as I dress for work, I will look into the mirror and say "I am blessed! I am enough! I am good!" Words cannot express how thankful I am.'

Rachel

'Bravo Marisa as you continue to develop ways to re-empower humanity and change the world—as this course and book definitely will.'

Karen

'I am enough in my strength, AND I am also enough when I am weak, or tired, or just "not feeling it today". I am enough when I do great things, AND when I merely do what I really must do today. I am enough when I am ready to take on the world, AND when I need a little emotional down time and space. Each day, I am enough..AND so are you.'

Theresa

'This is a lesson I never want to forget. While I still struggle with the bad habits of my subconscious thoughts, these three words give me perspective. These three words have also impacted the daughter of a friend of mine. When she found out why I had this on my wrist (and bathroom mirror), she took this message to her class at school. Her teacher now has this written on the board for all of the class to see each day.'

Steph

'Months ago when I "found" Marisa's info, I set a challenge for myself. I wrote it anytime I could, and used it as a response during each day. In 30 days I realized how positive my thinking had become and how thoughts in general were more productive and less comparing. *I Am Enough* says it all and I confirm the power of words. Thank you, Marisa Peer.'

Paige

'It's incredible how this quote works. Thank you Marisa.'

Susan

'It's been a year and I am still completely grateful and on cloud nine of how much my life has changed since taking Marisa's *I Am Enough* course! If it was possible for me it is possible for anyone. I came from a huge bankruptcy; I came from having to flee to the USA because of our life being in danger! You all can and you all are enough. Thank you Marisa.'

Vanessa

'I want to give this *I Am Enough* message 1000+ likes Marisa! Doing this training has changed my life and many of those around me. Thank you is not a big enough word to say how much I appreciate you and your gifts.'

Sum

'I don't recall anyone telling me openly that I wasn't enough, but I do recall being told that if I tried and just made a little more effort then, yes, I could really be good! Translation: You're O.K., but not quite enough. I realize that it's stayed with me all my life. I've done some quite lovely things in my life, but I could have done much more and with far more satisfaction if only I had heard *I Am Enough*. Time for change has come.'

Simon

'I have come to finally understand how *I Am Enough* shows up in my life, and when it doesn't. I've got the words on a sticky note on my monitor and I've become so much more confident in my own enoughness that I even speak differently. Thank you Marisa Peer for opening the door to greater understanding, healing and raising of the collective energies. As a mental health nurse I always found the medical model limited and restrictive. When I found Marisa and *I Am Enough* it made total sense. I have been using some of her methods with young people aged 13-19 with great results.'

Warren

"Write *I Am Enough* on all mirrors at home!" said my online coach Marisa Peer. This MINDSET work is the real deal. I realized then and there that "MY BIGGEST CONTRACEPTION TO SUCCESS (in life or in business) WERE MY OWN THOUGHTS." So now, when I work with entrepreneurs it is so easy to see that their biggest obstacles to success are not their products or services but their MINDSET which is set as: "I cannot achieve this/that", "I am a mom and I cannot run a successful business at the same time", "I am tired, I need X amount of sleep, otherwise I cannot function!", "I don't have enough time to do X". All of these things I said to myself for the past 12 years. I will tell you this over and over again: All of these words you are telling yourself and everyone around you have nothing to do with the words you are using. NOTHING. All of these sentences come from ONE SINGLE inside thought of self-doubt you tell yourself: "I am not enough". YOU ARE WRONG. I am proof. I was just like you. I went from a business dream to my dream business! Coz someone believed in me and told me *I Am Enough*.'

Lenja

'When learning *I Am Enough* years ago, it changed the way I viewed myself. This three letter word snapped me out of my lowest period of my life. Since then it's been my mantra. I am so glad I met you Marisa Peer.'

Nazia

'This whole course has been wonderful. I have to say it Marisa, you're beautiful. At 72 years young, I can assure you I've done many, many courses in my time and this beats them all. *I Am Enough* is just the most brilliant thing I've ever heard and I've loved it, loved it, loved it. I've got "I am enough" written all over the place and have just had it tattooed on my left hand. The whole course is truly transformational and worth every cent and minute spent on it. Thank you again Marisa for this wonderful course.'

Anon

'Lipstick on your mirror will change your life. *I Am Enough*—Marisa Peer, I love, love, love your work. It has changed my life in phenomenal ways. Thank you Marisa and I wish you the most extraordinary success with this book and the rest of your work.'

Angela

'I am doing *I Am Enough* program, which has been transformational for me. I am a completely different person than I was 6 months ago.'

Lorna

'I would like to share this amazing resolution with money blocks after 11 months. Yesterday I sold my house in Milan 250.000€ in just in 15 days. Thanks Marisa, *I Am Enough*, really works.'

Francesco

I Am Enough

Marisa Peer

ISBN-13: 978-1916411005
ISBN-10: 1916411002

DEDICATION

This book is dedicated to my parents Ron Peer and Dee Sadler and to beautiful Psalm Isadora. I miss you all so much.
"Unable to die are the loved for love is immortality."

It is also dedicated to my husband, John, who is my biggest support. I couldn't do what I do without you—you are my rock.

To my sister, Sian, who has made our business better than ever—you are, and always have been, indispensable.

To my gorgeous daughter, Phaedra Peer—my life is better every day because of you.

ACKNOWLEDGMENTS

A special thanks and acknowledgments to my wonderful friends Claudia, Dani, Helen and Maria—thank you for believing in me and supporting me.

To all the beautiful children in my life—Carylss, Lucas, Bree, Issac Freya, Jackson and Lola. You give me so much joy.

To Rosie Spinks, thank you for your help and input into this book. You are amazing and indispensable and I am so grateful for you.

To my own extraordinary teachers especially the late Gil Boyne David Viscott and Wayne Dyer, I appreciate your genius and I am honored to know you.

To my own clients over the years who have been so generous in sharing their stories and allowing them to be used in this book. I salute all of you for helping me to formulate techniques to create my own award-winning therapy that has helped so many people. Each of you played a part in the creation of Rapid Transformational Therapy

To my wonderful staff, amazing trainers, fabulous RTT therapists and gorgeous RTT students all over the world, who all come together to make our RTT training so amazing, so enjoyable and so powerful. I fall in love with you and the technique more with every single course we do and I am blown away by the privilege I have to teach this phenomenal method. I could not do it without each and every one of you. My deep and heartfelt thanks are not enough to express my gratitude and love for all of you. Thank you all for contributing to putting RTT on the map and making it the global powerhouse that it is becoming.

FOREWORD

I have known Marisa first professionally and then personally for over fifteen years and the day I met her was my lucky day. She is the most extraordinarily gifted therapist and I have sent her literally hundreds of people over the years, some international celebrities, some extremely famous, some a little bit famous and some not famous at all. They all had one thing in common: they needed help and I gave them her number knowing that she would change their life.

I can therefore easily say that her skills are unique and completely life-changing. Because of my high regard for her brilliant ability to change people's lives, and because of my job, I also gave her a significant role in one of my programs, Celebrity Fit Club, where she worked with eight celebrities over a four-month period and achieved extraordinary results. She is internationally considered to be the very best in her field and people travel from all over the world to seek her help. She is the only person I have ever met anywhere in the world who I know has the unique ability to help people with the widest assortment of problems, including those who have suffered the most severe forms of abuse, and achieve dramatic lifelong changes.

When people ask me why Marisa and her methods are different, that's easy. Here's what I say: When you have a heart problem, you go and talk to a heart specialist who diagnoses what is wrong and tells you that you need surgery. So, you go and have surgery. If you just talked and talked to the heart specialist, that heart problem would be diagnosed but untreated and at best remain the same, at worst get a whole lot more serious. With Marisa, she is both the specialist who diagnoses and the surgeon who operates. You talk, but then you dive deep and sort it out.

For every single person who reads this book it is their lucky day. Patterns and behaviors that make you unhappy do not need to stay that way forever. People tend to accept that they are hopeless at this or that, they tell you that they have "always" had relationships that go wrong, or do jobs they don't really enjoy - why?

Without even realizing it, people adapt to their negative patterns until those patterns rule them. When you feel like that, or when your brain feels like Spaghetti Junction, just read this book and feel the knots unknot.

The brain can change and is happy to, if you help it develop new neural pathways. This book is effortless to read and to do, and then in the days and weeks that follow you just feel totally changed.

I hope every person who reads this book allows it to help them change their life. Marisa is wonderful and so is this book.

Claudia Rosencrantz, Former ITV Controller of Entertainment

CONTENTS

To download the free hypnosis sessions which accompany the book, please visit: www.iamenough.com/resources

INTRODUCTION

In my long career as a therapist, thousands of people have walked into my office for thousands of different reasons. But of those thousands of clients, you may be surprised to learn that there are really only three types of people. That's right—only three.

It doesn't matter what the initiating problem, behavior, or issue is that a client has come to me to seek help for. It doesn't matter if they're a billionaire, an Olympian, a social hermit, a disabled veteran, a movie star, or just a regular office worker. It doesn't matter if they're British, Japanese, or Namibian; gay, straight, or transgendered; a high school dropout, a musical genius, or tax accountant. In spite of all these variables, by the end of each session, I have usually figured out which of the three archetypes they are.

Isn't that striking? That of all the diversity of human experience that people have today, we can all be boiled down to just three types. You are probably wondering what those types are, but before I tell you, I want to tell you something more important. I want to tell you *why that's true*.

The traditional field of psychology likes to make things complicated. However, in my experience, there has been one core tenet which has informed my practice as an internationally-renowned therapist, and it is incredibly simple. This laser-sharp focus on simplicity often goes against the grain, clinically speaking. However, I can tell you with certainty that it's been the reason why I'm commonly referred to as the "therapist's therapist"—or the person that other practitioners send their clients to when they're struggling to get results with them. It's also the reason I've gained a reputation for helping clients in one or two sessions, rather than years of repeated visits.

So, what is this insight I've spent 30 years and thousands of hours of practice learning? It is my understanding that humans come onto this planet with two powerful emotional needs: to find connection, and to avoid rejection. If you dig deep enough into the emotional problems of almost anyone, you can trace their issues back to a lack of fulfilment of those two needs. It's really that simple because that truth is so powerful and part of its strength is its simplicity.

If you want proof of just how fundamental these needs are, our society provides plenty of extreme examples. Take a look at someone in the most extreme form of social isolation we've come up with: solitary confinement. Numerous studies in the United States have shown that solitary confinement is one of the most damaging and irreversible punishments to bestow on a criminal, no matter what they've done. Symptoms that are known to be caused by solitary confinement include hallucinations, panic attacks, depression, loss of memory and mood swings. Tellingly, the four percent of inmates in American prisons who are subjected to solitary confinement make up 50 percent of the total suicides in the incarceration system. All of this tells us that a human can have no direct threat to their survival in terms of their biological needs— food, shelter, oxygen—but if they feel rejected by society and are unable to forge a human connection of any kind, they are in the worst kind of poverty we know. It is a poverty of the spirit.

Similarly, if you ask a homeless person what the worst part of being homeless is, the answer they give often isn't what you'd expect. They don't say that they miss having their own bed or a steak dinner (though I'm sure they do miss those things), they say the constant feeling of being ignored and rejected by society at large is too much to bear. Walk into a soup kitchen and you'll often find people are there for a chat with someone even more so than for the soup. It's also been proven that one of the major factors causing drug addiction and alcoholism is the feeling of not belonging and one of the successes of AA is that it allows addicts to feel a sense of connection with each other.

You see, to a certain extent we all still have the mindset of tribal times. When we lived in interdependent tribal structures, it was imperative that we didn't get rejected by our brethren as no human could survive in the wilderness out on their own. In that case, rejection really did mean death and connection meant survival. That is why this fear is so deeply rooted and the cause of so many of our modern problems.

As I've developed my rapid transformational hypnotherapy methods—which now form the basis of my international course for my Rapid Transformational Therapy, or RTT, method—I've always come back to this fundamental truth: more than anything else we need connection and we avoid rejection. And when I'm trying to figure out which of the three types my client fits into, it's always through the lens of these dual desires.

Three types of clients

You are probably wondering just what are the three categories that I've managed to separate my clients into, without much deviation. The first type of client is a person who would love to have it all—loving relationships, a great job, financial security, and self-love, confidence, and inner peace—but can't manage to attain any of it, let alone hang on to it. The second type of client is one who has many of those things described above but is sabotaging them in major or minor ways such as addiction, workaholism, or cheating on their spouse. And the third type, the rarest type of client who *does* manage, through working on their mindset, to attain it all—relationship, health, career calling, well-being, inner peace—is working on their ability to share it with other people.

For some people, these categories may seem crude or too simplistic. But because I've seen the transformation of the first two types after applying my methods, I'm confident that it really is this simple. It all goes back to that fundamental truth I shared. Feeling disconnected or rejected can lead to all sorts of issues that manifest in the types of clients who belong in groups one and two. That rejection and disconnection can come from parental estrangement, being bullied, having a disability or never feeling that you were safe. It can manifest as a fear of intimacy, an inflated ego, or an addiction to eating, alcohol or drugs. Indeed, it doesn't matter *where* the rejection or lack of connection comes from, it almost *always* leads to a person who feels as though certain things in life will never be available to them. And many modern-day ailments are a function of humans trying to fill the resulting emptiness or gap that they feel.

In about 2012, it became so apparent to me that the third group of clients—the ones who had it all and wanted to share it—were operating on a different level of consciousness and self-love. They didn't just feel, they knew that everything was available to them. This wasn't because they had experienced perfect, trauma-free lives. Quite the contrary. It was because of how they had changed their mindsets.

I was so struck by the stand-out nature of this third group that I resolved to find a way to teach not just the first two groups of clients, but all my followers and readers all over the world how they could become the third type. This book, along with my RTT course, is my attempt to do just that. I want everyone to know that it's not only possible to get over their problems, issues, and hang-ups to live a full and happy life—it's theirs for the taking once they can get their mind on their side by effectively dialoguing with it.

When you like yourself, your life is extraordinary

As I said before, there are many reasons why people from all walks of life feel disconnected and rejected. In a lot of cases, these reasons start very early on in life, before we are even aware of our own consciousness. Maybe your father was never home, and when he was, he commented on your weight. Maybe your mother could only be pleased if you were perfect, and so you never felt you measured up despite your hardest efforts. Or maybe you were the victim of trauma or abuse before you even knew what those words were. All of those represent rejection to varying degrees. As we age, we wonder why we have the same stubborn problems such as relationship sabotage, addiction, weight problems, lack of motivation, or fear of commitment following us around. In a great many cases, these issues turn into a kind of self-loathing, a resignation to the fact that we will never be who we want to be. Our conscious mind just assumes it is our own fault: that we are lazy, we aren't good enough, we simply can't change it, that this is how life will always be. Meanwhile, our harder-to-reach subconscious mind is often still stewing in the deep root causes of rejection and disconnection, agnostic to what is going on up at the surface level.

As a therapist, I meet so many people who don't like themselves and, by extension, they create lives they don't like either. The third group of clients are the ones that do like themselves. That's not because they are perfect, or had perfect parents, or have experienced no adversity; it's because they have learned how to self-dialogue and redirect their insecurities and fears around rejection and disconnection into a tremendous self-belief.

This isn't the same as ego or narcissism; it's a sense of radical self-love. It's a stated, embedded, unshakable belief in the worthiness of one's self. With it, I truly believe you can do anything. Without it, you will stay in group one or two, with your subconscious mind sabotaging you every step of the way, always feeling that you are not quite good enough no matter what your accomplishments are or how many other people value you.

The chapters of this book are devoted to teaching you how to attain that unshakeable belief in yourself—the radical act of simply liking yourself—so you can join the third group of clients. This isn't so you can be superior or better than everyone else, but rather so that you, too, can help spread this message of self-love that can change the world. It's information that I believe everyone should know, but it isn't taught in schools because so many educators haven't yet learned it themselves. I like to think it is my purpose in life to spread it to as many people as possible because I have seen the life-changing effects of this method in my practice, in emails from my readers, on stage when I speak at conferences, and in my training course.

The chapters will take you through various techniques which you can apply to your everyday life, starting right away. They aren't bizarre or difficult to implement, and they don't cost money or require special equipment. All you need is a willingness to change and to address the mental habits you've been stuck with for ages.

The first chapter will explore how your speech and outer dialogue affect what your mind thinks it wants you to do, while the second chapter will explore visualization and how imagery affects our beliefs. The third chapter will elucidate how to forever alter your feelings towards things you don't like, such as phobias, dieting, or hard work. Chapters Four through Six will share some of the simple but effective habits that almost all successful people I've treated over the years practice in their everyday lives. Chapter Seven will address how you can apply some of those habits to a challenge that many people face: weight loss. Chapter Eight will reveal the mantra that I believe can heal people while Chapter Nine will explore how to operate in a world that will not always be kind to you. Chapter Ten will deal with the romantic relationships in your life, and the final chapter will teach you how to put all those lessons together to create a wonderful life.

As you can see, none of these techniques are about avoiding adversity or making your life conflict free. None of them are quick fixes, based on bogus ideas, or New Age woo woo either. Rather, they are all about equipping your brain to deal with what life hands you in a way that is self-directed, filled with gratitude, and not at the whim of your mind's worst habits. It's important to accept that we very often cannot change the external events that surround us, we can only change how we respond to them. Fortunately, though, changing how you feel on the inside will change how you feel about your external events more than you could ever imagine.

I can't tell you how many people's lives I've seen change by adopting these techniques. To the outside world, they may have lost a ton of weight, started a wildly successful business, finally found a loving relationship, and patched up their relationship with their parents. But in all those cases, what's really happened is that they've changed how they relate to themselves. Their inner world has become a lot more loving and, in turn, their outer world has changed for the better. I'm here to teach you the easy but effective methods that will lead you to this "I am enough" life. It's not magic, but it will have a magical effect on your life.

There is a metaphor I love to use when it comes to training your mind to work for you, not against you. I want you to think of your subconscious mind as a wild horse. It's running through fields, without restraint, letting its power and might overpower any impediment or barrier. Meanwhile, your conscious mind is the horse trainer. It is possible to train a wild horse like this to become obedient and docile, but you would need an extremely experienced horse trainer to do it successfully; an amateur just won't do. The same goes for your mind. Most people go through their lives as an amateur horse trainer with a wild black stallion on their hands. For those people, the wild horse—their subconscious mind—controls them, not the other way around. They wonder why, over and over, they struggle with the same hang-ups and bad habits. The reason is that you simply can't control your mind unless you know exactly what to do with it. With this book, I intend to teach you exactly that, and in turn allow you to have everything, keep everything, and enjoy and share it, too.

A note about how to use this book

This book encapsulates much of what I've learned in my thirty years as a therapist, author, and speaker, working with thousands of clients, and reaching many more readers, followers, and audiences all over the world. Working with, and hearing feedback from, all these unique people over the years, I have learned that while different things work for different people, a single, simple mantra such as "I am enough" can be the life-changing ingredient to forever alter their inner dialogue. For others, establishing a new habit around how they approach tasks they hate doing can be the difference between finding wild success for their business, or not.

That's why the best way to use this book is the way that feels right for you. If some chapters speak to you more than others, then I encourage you to read and re-read those until you have fully instilled their teachings into your subconscious mind.

Occasionally, throughout the book, I will refer to hypnotic audio recordings that you can use to help bolster and strengthen the teachings in these pages. There are two powerful hypnotic audios provided. They can be found here: www.iamenough.com/resources.

Audio One - The Healing Vortex
This audio is designed to help you balance your body and to overcome emotional and even physical issues by setting off a powerful healing response. Of course all healing is self-healing and by repeated playing of this audio you can implement powerful healing within you.

Audio Two - I Am Enough

This audio is to instill and code into you the unshakable knowing that you're enough. The more you play it the more it will become a part of who you are, so enjoy playing it frequently.

I recommend you play each of these audios for 21 days in succession in order to code and wire in the powerful message contained. After 21 days continue to play them at least once a month or as often as you desire to keep that message at the forefront of your mind.

If you've never been hypnotized before, don't worry. The instructions are quite simple and hearing these words over at least a three-week period will create the opportunity for my messages to stay in your mind. N.B. hypnosis is perfectly safe and natural and nothing untoward can happen to you while in this state nor can you be made to do anything against your will nor can you remain stuck in hypnosis.

If you're worried about falling asleep during hypnosis, or you feel it makes you sleepy, don't feel stressed about that either. Hypnosis and sleep are actually quite similar, as in both states your subconscious mind is working more than your conscious mind. All you need to do at the outset of a hypnosis session is make sure you're comfortable, in a quiet place, with the phone disconnected or your mobile phone switched off. To begin, simply close your eyelids but try to have your eyeballs looking up towards your eyebrows. You will notice your eyelids start fluttering, which is exactly what you want. Take deep breaths and simply relax into the recording and follow what it tells you to do from there.

Don't worry if you feel like you're not doing it "right." There is no wrong way. Just remember that my hypnosis won't send you to sleep—it will wake you up. Just relax and you'll find you get more comfortable as you go.

CHAPTER ONE
Hell Is Not Your Morning Commute

The greatest discovery of my generation is that human beings can alter their lives by altering their attitudes of mind.
William James, US Psychologist

When I was training to be a therapist, I was challenged when my teacher said to me, "The mind is really complicated and very complex. It takes a lifetime to understand and to master." I immediately thought, "Well, how is that going to work then? No one has got a lifetime to master their mind." Furthermore, what is the point of being 80 years old before you can finally work out your mind? That is not helpful. And guess what? It's actually not true either.

The truth is that the human mind has one simple job: to keep you alive as long as possible. To do that, our mind is an expert at helping us avoid and flee what causes us pain or danger.

When we were living in tribes in the bush, this job was actually quite difficult. We had to flee predators, find water and food, and protect ourselves from the elements constantly. We were under physical threat far more often than we are today, and we were designed to respond to those stressors. Our bodies developed "fight or flight" responses which informed how we responded in times of stress, which usually involved large animals, angry tribesmen, or natural disasters.

The physical world has changed a lot since then. On a daily basis, most people in the modern world don't have a direct threat to their physical well-being. But there's a fundamental design flaw here: our brain hasn't changed much at all to reflect our new, safer and more tame reality. We are still primed for fight or flight responses to the stress and adversity life throws our way. The difference now is that the stressors and roadblocks are less primal and more mental. Nevertheless, when we come onto the planet, our mind still believes in its one, singular job: keeping us alive. And how does it do that? By listening to the instructions we give it about what causes us pain.

This is why, when we're sitting in traffic in the morning, running late to work, and we spill our coffee all down our white shirt we say, "This commute is killing me. This traffic is a nightmare. My boss is stressing me out. I'm dying under the pressure," our brain *actually believes us*. And so how does our body respond to these instructions? Well, it's been told we're under threat—something is killing you! Your brain wants to keep you alive! So your heart rate goes up, your cortisol levels increase, your body surges with hormones, you feel angry and lash out at your kid sitting in the back seat and send a rude text message to your colleague. We tell our brain that it's stressed and that we're under direct threat, and lo and behold, it *believes us*. Hour after hour, day after day, our brain uses the language it hears us using to inform how it should feel.

This is the first important lesson I want you to learn: Your mind does what it thinks you want it to do and what it truly believes is in your best interest.

In the moment you're sitting in traffic and allowing yourself to feel immense stress, your body is desperately trying to get you out of that situation because you are giving it all the indicators that sitting in the car is causing you great pain. You are giving your mind instructions, through your words, that are triggering a physical fight or flight response. But the truth is, being 15 minutes late to work in a stained white shirt doesn't actually cause you any pain. Inconvenience, perhaps, but not the kind of stress one feels when their house is burning down or they're being chased by a wild boar. But your mind doesn't care. You've verbally expressed that you're in pain and under threat, and thus, your brain gives you all the symptoms and responses to help you flee it. The result? You just end up stressed and miserable.

Like all my teachings, this truth is based on science. Muscle testing is a technique that comes from the field of applied kinesiology. In a sense, muscle testing is like asking your subconscious mind a question with words and getting a physical answer from your body. Muscle testing proves that our bodies respond to words in a way we're not always conscious of, or in control of, similar to what happens when we're sitting in traffic that we verbally call "hell on earth."

I Am Enough

Exercise

Do this now: Test yourself with a statement that is untrue (you will need someone else to assist you). Put out your arm and hold it very straight and make a fist. Have a friend push down on your arm. Your job is to resist the pushing, keep your arm as strong as you can and not allow them to lower your arm. Once you have established your strength you now repeat out loud words that are true such as:

"I am female" or "My name is Amanda," then repeat the pushing exercise.

You will notice that your arm remains very strong and upright when you say something that is positive and truthful.

Now repeat the exercise saying something that is obviously untrue, such as: "I am a male", "My name is Voltarol".

As you say something negative and incorrect, your body will have a "weak" response—your arm will not be able to resist the person who is administering the pushing.

If you say something true, however, your body will have a strong response and will be able to resist.

Remember that words are powerful, and your mind is always listening. Every word you say becomes a blueprint that your mind and body work to meet and turn into your reality. The strongest force in you is that you must act in a way that consistently matches your thinking. Once you have proof of this it becomes easy to pay more attention to your words and to make your words more positive, so that you are positively influencing the blueprint you are constantly working towards. This is a wonderful thing to do with children because it really teaches them the power of their own words and thoughts.

Muscle testing works with anyone. If you want to test out the truth that your mind responds to the words you tell it, try the next exercise:

Exercise

Using your own fingers create a circle with your thumb and finger on one hand.

I want you to start pulling against the circle with the thumb and finger of your other hand just to see that you're very strong. Keep pulling and resisting against the circle you made and at the same time say out loud:

"I'm super successful and extraordinary. I'm super successful and extraordinary."

Notice how the circle remains unbroken because your resistance is strong.

Now I want you to say:

"I'm a loser, and I mess everything up. I'm a loser, and I mess everything up."

What happens as you say, "I'm a loser. I'm a loser. I mess everything up" is that you're losing your strength, losing your grip. Then go back to saying, "I'm extraordinary. I'm successful. I'm awesome." Every muscle in your body is responding to the words you make and the thoughts you think.

The lesson, of course, is to be far more careful about what you think and the words you use.

This exercise is even better if you have another person pull against your closed fingers whilst you make statements both good and bad.

Throw out your mind's old instruction manual

So now that we know our mind is listening closely to our words to inform our physical actions and how we feel, what can we do with that information? The answer is profound.

Think about something in your life that has always caused you conflict, pain, or stress. Maybe it's losing weight—something we'll discuss at length in Chapter Seven—which you seem to sabotage no matter how hard you try. Or perhaps you become incredibly nervous at the prospect of public speaking, even though your failure to master it is preventing you from getting a promotion. Maybe you just can't stick to a new habit such as writing every day or exercising, despite the fact that your conscious mind loves the idea of establishing this habit.

The reason for these sticking points we all have as adults is most likely due to old instructions your mind once received. Let's use the example of public speaking.

One of the things I've learned in my decades of private practice is that the fear of speaking in front of a crowd—whether it's 20 people or 2,000—is the most commonly held fear among human beings. That's because public speaking carries with it an inherent vulnerability: the risk of rejection and ostracism from the crowd. And remember what we're all on the planet trying to avoid? Rejection.

For people who will do anything to avoid standing up in front of a crowd and making themselves vulnerable, there is very often an incident or series of incidences in their past where they felt taunted, teased, or rejected. Maybe they forgot the words to the play in the school talent show, and the school bullies teased them. Maybe they had a speech impediment as a child and were unfairly called upon by a teacher who hoped to cure it. Or maybe they simply never felt *accepted* by friends and peers early on in life, so as an adult they desperately minimize any chance they might be further rejected. Now, 30 years later, there are no school bullies and their inability to deliver a presentation without immense nerves, sweating, and stammering is the thing that's actually causing them pain and preventing them getting a pay rise. But once again, the brain is doing what it thinks you want it to do: avoiding the pain of rejection by avoiding public speaking at all costs.

Want more proof that your mind listens to your words for instructions? Just look at this behavior from a positive viewpoint. Think of the way that US Marines can run mile after mile in heavy boots, carrying weighty equipment, with a sense of ease and even enjoyment. They can do this because the camaraderie and positivity they create by chanting motivating slogans and songs while they trudge through the mud makes their mind believe *they want to be there*. All of a sudden, running ten miles in harsh conditions doesn't cause them pain, but rather valor and honor. Similarly, look at the way that someone can happily sit to get their entire body tattooed. They ignore the pain because they've told their mind they *want* the end product. Their mind does not see this pain as a threat to their survival or safety, so it happily plays along and allows them to be punctured by needles without fleeing.

Once you realize that your mind responds to the detailed instructions you give it through your own inner and outer dialogue, you can use that information to your advantage. However, I want to be clear: this is not about "the power of positive thinking," where people are instructed to simply pretend everything is rosy and perfect in the wake of fears, phobias, and adversity. Rather, it's about giving your mind more specific, direct, and up to date communication around those fears, phobias, and moments of challenge.

When this logic is applied, your "nightmarish, torturous" commute becomes "an inconvenient but surmountable challenge." The Sunday afternoon you have to miss a party to spend at home working on your accounts or writing a proposal doesn't have to be "the last thing you feel like doing ever" but rather "an opportunity to get ahead and feel ready for the week ahead." The new dialogue you give your mind doesn't have to be unrealistic or a fantasy— after all, nobody likes being in traffic or missing out on weekend fun—but it does need to be a reframing of your actual reality. Unless your life is actually under threat, don't give your mind the cues that it needs to plunge into fight or flight mode each time something doesn't go exactly as planned.

It can often seem utterly daunting to change the habits and thought patterns we've had our entire lives. I like to think of it as "updating our software." Just as our laptops and smartphones have bugs and vulnerabilities that coders address with each new software update so, too, does our mind. If you don't update your laptop, it is vulnerable to viruses and begins running slowly and inefficiently. The same can be said of your mind. When you feel there is a sticking point in your life—and it doesn't matter what it is—it is helpful to find the root cause or the outdated information. Figuring out what that is allows you to update the instructions you give your mind, just as you update your software.

Hypnosis can be immensely helpful in this regard as it can quickly and effectively take you back to the moment that you gave your mind these outdated, unhelpful beliefs and reverse them. A useful metric when it comes to updating our beliefs is that it takes between ten days and twenty-one days to let go of an old belief and replace it with a new, better one. In the grand scheme of things, that's not so long for a belief you've held onto for thirty years. So, give yourself some leeway in instilling the new instructions you have for your mind.

For everyone who has struggled to overcome unhelpful and negative belief systems that can leave you feeling depressed, anxious, sad, isolated, as well as physically impacting your body, the knowledge that your own mind is able to change these beliefs very quickly once you know how (and this book shows you how) is good news. Your life will never be perfect—nobody's is—but the way you respond to the imperfections and adversity that do come your way can be more sophisticated than a caveman being chased by a saber-toothed tiger. Give your mind the intelligible, reasonable, up to date and non-dramatic information it needs to keep your problems and challenges in perspective, and you'll find your life will become much, much easier and so much more enjoyable. Never forget, you make your beliefs and habits—and then they turn around and make you. So, choose wisely and give your mind better instructions so it knows better how to respond.

CHAPTER TWO
Why Babies Aren't Afraid Of Flying

The feeling that cannot find its expression in tears may cause other organs to weep.
Henry Maudsley, Psychiatrist

Whenever I'm about to board a plane, I always look around me to see if there are any babies in the departure lounge. If there are, I love observing the way they are carried onto an airplane with little to no understanding and oblivious to the fact that they are about to be catapulted thousands of feet into the air in an aluminum tube. Like almost all infants, they are that beautiful blend of both helpless and carefree. They have such blind trust in their parents or carers and, thus, have no reason to think that they might be led into something they should fear.

When I have clients who fear flying, as often happens, I encourage them to engage in this observational exercise, too. Examining how babies behave in certain circumstances where adults struggle is instructive in so many ways. The reason for this is that babies still have something we were all born with, but often lose: the birthright of confidence. Unless they are in direct pain or discomfort, babies don't cry. They don't create false realities, project about what the future will bring, or feel fearful of things that haven't happened yet, be it a plane crash, an exam, or a presentation at work. They simply judge their feelings by exactly what's happening to them in the present moment.

Here's a secret for you, one that might just change your life: You can be exactly that way, too.

It's so simple, yet true. Everything you've feel is the result of just two things:

1. The pictures you make in your head.
2. The words you say to yourself.

What most people don't understand is that you have full power and control to choose better words and pictures—not just sometimes but all the time. This is what very successful people naturally do because they already understand that we have the power to create those words and pictures—you're doing it constantly without even realizing it. After all, we all talk to ourselves continually and fill our minds with images. What I am helping you to do is to fill up your mind with better words and images and notice the consistently better response you get.

Often, when a person is afraid of flying it's because they are afraid of being out of control. The fact that they daily engage in other activities that involve risk (such as driving a car or crossing the road) doesn't matter to them. Fear is not a logical thought process for most people, so even the most convincing statistics don't apply here. The lack of control triggers a raft of negative mental images in their brain. I've heard clients, who are fearful flyers, refer to an airplane as a "flying coffin" and a "death trap". With words and mental imagery as strong and specific as that, it's no wonder that they fear boarding the plane!

Here's another secret: The physical experience of anxiety and stress—quickened heart rate, butterflies, inability to focus—is almost identical to the physical experience of excitement. Whenever you feel nervous, you can choose the emotion and instruct your mind about the feelings you are experiencing. For a woman afraid of flying, she can just as easily convince her mind she's on a roller coaster or at a fun fair, and all of a sudden, the prospect of flying goes from being associated with death to being associated with childhood days spent at Disneyland. She still doesn't have control over what happens, but the terrifying pictures about losing that control are gone. That's why I often say that getting around strong phobias like this is as simple as what I call the "lie, cheat, and steal" method:

Lie to your mind, cheat fear, and steal back the phenomenal confidence you were born with.

Now, I know what you're thinking: This is too good to be true. How can someone who is terrified of flying simply flip the script—"I'm not in a flying coffin, I'm on a roller coaster ride!"—and reverse years of abject terror. It may sound far-fetched, until you consider that these kinds of mind tricks surround us every day. You are doing them without even realizing it.

Take, for instance, a cheeseburger. Four people can have remarkably different feelings towards this cheeseburger, despite the fact that their bodies would have more or less the same reaction to it: to digest it. Someone with an active eating disorder might feel abject fear at the prospect of eating a cheeseburger full of calories, while someone who is a vegetarian might feel indignant outrage at the ethics of eating an animal. Similarly, a Hindu might feel great sadness that a sacred being has been killed for a meal, and a hungry carnivore who hasn't eaten all day might feel excitement and joy. All of these people biologically have the same relationship to the cheeseburger: their body craves the fat and calorically dense food that we're conditioned to enjoy because, as we'll discuss further in Chapter Six, these foods were once scarce when we were hunter gatherers. But the picture each of these people have constructed is drastically different, and that picture directly informs how they feel about it.

Another example is the well-documented placebo effect. If someone *thinks* their body is being given life-saving or curative medicine, their body will do some of the work of making the patient feel better, even if all they're being given is a sugar pill. This is not fantasy, but a well-documented effect that proves your brain has tremendous power that is dependent on what it believes. Need another example? What about a needle: A heroin addict has no qualms about injecting a needle into their arm because they've associated it with something they desperately want and need. Meanwhile, many other people could hardly get a vaccine administered by a nurse, let alone do it themselves. The needle itself is agnostic to our feelings and has the same physical effect on all of us. Its power over us has to do with how we think about the needle.

One of my favorite scientific examples that documents the idea that words and pictures we tell ourselves inform our reality comes from the education sector. Numerous studies have shown that if teachers are told their students are "gifted," the way in which they teach those children changes, and thus the overall results of the classroom improve. Of course, the students don't have to be gifted, they can be a mix of average, below average and gifted. But if teachers believe that the children are gifted, overall results for all the students will improve.

One influential study was conducted by psychologist Robert Rosenthal as early as the 1960s. America's National Public Radio wrote about his seminal findings: "As Rosenthal did more research, he found that expectations affect teachers' moment-to-moment interactions with the children they teach in a thousand almost invisible ways. Teachers give the students that they expect to succeed more time to answer questions, more specific feedback, and more approval: They consistently touch, nod and smile at those kids more."

Lie, Cheat, and Steal

If you can lie to your brain about a cheeseburger, or a needle, or a sugar pill, you can do it with the more important things in your life, too.

The first thing you need to really understand in order to lie, cheat, and steal your way to a happy mind and a happy you is this:

If you use the wrong words, you create the wrong reality.

Most people don't realize they have a choice in the matter because, as humans, we are unfortunately hard-wired to be attuned to what might go wrong. The reason is because it was evolutionarily beneficial for us to do so. As Oliver Burkeman once wrote in the Guardian: "This is what makes bad news especially compelling: In our evolutionary past, it was a very good thing that your attention could be easily seized by negative information, since it might well indicate an imminent risk to your own survival. (The cave-dweller who always assumed there was a lion behind the next rock would usually be wrong but he'd be much more likely to survive and reproduce than one who always assumed the opposite.)" That is exactly why it is easier to be negative than positive; once upon a time we were more likely to survive if we were negative. Even today we could say strapping on a seat belt is negative because it means we are expecting to crash but the seat belt is making us more likely to survive. The very good news is we no longer need to be negative to survive. We can choose to be positive and choose to have a happier and more productive life.

There is no longer an imminent risk to our survival around every corner—flying, for example, is statistically safer than crossing a city street—but our brains still believe it's true. But here's the thing that all successful people I know have figured out: We can choose to actively counter our inclination to expect the worst and expect the best instead (or at least a more manageable version of what we're actually going through). Whether it's a layoff from work, an airplane ride, or an unexpected illness, you largely can't control the external forces that influence your life, but you can choose the beliefs, words, and mindset that you respond to these factors with. This is not fantasy or meaningless positive thinking. The reason this seems "too good to be true" is that the vast majority of people go through life not knowing this.

I often have clients and readers who say: "Sure, Marisa, changing beliefs through visualizing different pictures may work for other people, but it doesn't work for me. I've tried it." To those people I sometimes say: "Well lucky you! That means you are always free of fear, anxiety, and shame. As all of those emotions come from negative visualizations." Of course, they quickly realize that they are visualizing realities all day in their lives—"I'm going to mess that up, this job is so stressful, my children are making me crazy, this plane is going to crash"—they just don't realize those visualizations are affecting them negatively.

Just like we learn from the carefree baby in the departure lounge: You can't worry if you don't visualize negative pictures in your head. Some people believe that they can't visualize at all but you would never find your car in a car park nor even find your way home if you could not visualize. We all visualize continually—all you have to do is visualize *better* by visualizing positive outcomes. That in itself can dramatically improve your happiness level.

Chances are, you already are lying to your mind in a negative fashion, so let's have an example of how you can use this technique to *positively* influence your life. I used to have a client who was, quite simply, utterly overwhelmed by her life. Her children were overbearing, her husband unhelpful, and her job left her feeling overstretched and under-appreciated each and every day. As I sat through our session, I paid very close attention to the language she was using. She repeatedly said: "I can't cope. I can't cope with my badly behaved children, I can't cope with how impossible my job is, I can't cope with my constantly chaotic household."

After she finished talking, I pointed out to her that she was frequently using the phrase: "I can't cope." Immediately, she broke down: "Oh my goodness, my mother used to say that constantly." This client had inherited that phrase—and by extension, that belief—from her mother, and was not taking responsibility for the words and pictures she was choosing. As a result, she had convinced herself that her life was one she could not cope with.

So, we replaced that phrase: "I can't cope" with something more neutral: "I have phenomenal coping skills." Every time she began to feel overwhelmed in her life, I instructed her to say out loud or to herself: "I have phenomenal coping skills." This subtle shift slowly made her believe the phrase was true. By using different words, she created a different picture. In a few weeks, she came back feeling far less overwhelmed by her life, succeeding in her job, and getting on better with her kids and husband, who had noticed a shift in her. But her life hadn't changed at all—her beliefs about it had, which made it all the more bearable. She was a perfect example of the fact that in order to underachieve you have to fill your mind with negative thoughts and images, and to overachieve you simply have to do the opposite.

Notice here that I didn't instruct my client to say something that wasn't true. Her job was hard, and her kids were a challenge. But by changing the overtly negative: "My job is hell, my kids are rude and badly behaved" to a more neutral, realistic version of events: "My job is demanding at times and my kids can be a challenge, but I have phenomenal coping skills," you create less emotion-charged feelings towards it. This isn't about the power of positive thinking and pretending everything is rosy. It's about actively reframing the events of your life to reflect a different, more realistic picture.

So, "I'm late again, I've really messed up, everything is going to go wrong today," turns into: "I prefer to be on time, but I can still do this. I can get through the day in a manageable fashion." With the latter phrase, you're not pretending you're superman or superwoman, but you are encouraging yourself to not expect the worst.

One of my clients had a phobia that was so extreme she was hospitalized. On her release, as part of her outpatients treatment, she attended group therapy and would sit in a circle with other patients and each had to say something positive. She would tell me that they all said something along the lines of: "today I saw some daffodils and I felt better." At her turn she would follow their lead and say: "butterflies make me feel calm," or something similar. I told her she was not giving her mind clear directions to curtail her anxiety and at the next therapy meeting, when it was her turn, I asked her to say out loud, "I have phenomenal coping skills." The following week she was to say, "I have extraordinary coping skills," then "I have exemplary coping skills," and then, "I have outstanding coping skills."

Not only did she report that she felt much better, she also reported other patients asking if they could share her message and then the therapist wrote those words on the board and commented that this group was making the fastest progress in recovering.

This was of course because they gave their mind clear instructions. Saying out loud to themselves and others, "I have extraordinary coping skills," gives the mind a very clear instruction and direction; it gives it the blueprint to move towards, whereas saying, "I like butterflies," does not. What you present to your mind, your mind will then present back to you. It all starts with your words which you have the power to change.

You'll remember that in the Introduction, I spoke about the three types of clients I see. Taking responsibility for the words and pictures in your head is perhaps the biggest thing that separates the first two types—who don't have what they want—from the third type: the ones that do. The fact is that most of the clients I see every day are not aware that how they feel about the world around them is influenced by choices they are making.

Exercise

What I want you to do is name that chatter or that internal voice. Personify it as a kind of cartoon villain if you need to, but the point of this trick is to see that chatter and thoughts are not inextricably part of *you*.

They are an external force that you can rid from your mind. By saying:

"Oh, there's the Joker again, coming back right when I don't need him."

By kicking him out of your thought patterns you are acknowledging you have power over those thoughts.

By accepting that your negativity doesn't have to be *who you* are, but rather, an unhelpful habit you can get rid of, you can begin to replace the Joker with something else. You can even give the negative part a name, like Susie or Kevin. The ability to recognize it, laugh about it and, most important of all, change it is so transformational.

It's important that I provide my readers with practical ways to implement these changes. When it comes to lying to your mind, it can be helpful to personify the unhelpful thoughts and the way you talk to yourself—what you might call your internal chatter. So, let's say that each and every time you start to try and change your negative thought patterns, your mind takes over and insists on reintroducing negativity and unhelpful words and pictures into your head.

Who might that something else be? Just as I did with my client who insisted she couldn't cope, pay close attention to the words and phrases you're constantly saying to yourself. Once you've identified some repeat offenders, ask yourself: Would you talk to your best friend that way? Would you say: "Oh, you're always messing things up," "You're so hopeless," or "You really have taken on way too much, you'll never get it all done."

Chances are, if you're a good friend, you wouldn't dream of saying those things; you would be kind and encouraging and helpful. As a friend, you might say: "Life isn't perfect but we all do the best we can," or "I'm sure you'll get through it, and I'll help you get there." So, ask yourself what might happen if you choose to talk to yourself as you might address a friend. Be kind and encouraging and supportive to *yourself* and you'll be amazed at how much easier the world around you seems to become.

Let's imagine a day in the life of you before you implement a better dialogue with yourself:

You wake up, look in a mirror and begin to criticize and berate yourself because you forgot to sew the loose hem on your suit. Not only do you say, "I should have hemmed that and now I don't have time," you add, "I am such an idiot, I am a loser," "this shirt looks too tight. I should have lost weight. I am hopeless/pathetic/ a waste of space," etc, etc.
You look in the fridge and you are out of healthy food and reduced to eating white carbs and sugar, so for the second time in ten minutes you call yourself an idiot, a retard, a moron, stupid.

As your morning progresses you call yourself more names for forgetting to charge your phone/ not leaving enough time to get to your destination/ not having the right amount of change for your ride/ not preparing fully for your meeting/ not doing a good enough job at work/ yelling at a colleague/ not having any healthy snacks so when your meeting runs late you eat pizza. On your way home you beat yourself up for leaving too late to avoid the traffic/ you give yourself so much grief for missing the gym because you are too tired to go, too tired to cook so you eat cereal and berate yourself even more for being a lazy, out of shape loser. Finally, the cute person you have been chatting to online ghosts you tonight and you justify it by adding, "I knew that would happen. What have I got to offer someone like them? They would have got bored with me anyway so I'm not surprised. I'm useless, fat and stupid."

You may think I am exaggerating, yet clients come sit in my chair and I ask them, "How was your weekend?" and they often reply, "Lousy, my date cancelled on me. I know it's because they found someone better so I ate like a pig non stop all weekend and now I am the size of a house. I'm just a hot mess and a train wreck." None of this is true; the date may have picked up their low sense of self-worth and been put off by it (both sexes find confidence immensely sexy and neediness a turn off) or they may have had a crisis to deal with. Regardless, the client could not have eaten non stop all weekend, they did not eat like a pig, they are not the size of a house or a hot mess or a train wreck but when you describe yourself like this you set yourself up to feel bad, and it's so painful and so unnecessary.

Imagine now if it was not you, but your best friend who spoke to you like that and threw those insulting hurtful names and labels at you all day and every day. Wouldn't you want to kick them out of your life forever and get better friends?

It's time for you to be a better friend to *you* by ending all the self-criticism and name calling.

You can choose whether to be negative and critical about yourself or positive and full of praise. Your mind does not know, and indeed it does not care, if what you tell it is right or wrong, good or bad, true or false, helpful or very unhelpful—it just lets it in. Your mind's job is to act on the words you tell it and to use those words to form a blueprint that it must take you towards. Your job is to give your mind much more powerful, descriptive and positive words. Your mind is doing its job, so do your job and give it better instructions all the time.

One more thing—you do have a choice, we always have a choice. You can choose to be negative, use negative language and feel lousy because of it or you can choose to be positive, use positive language and notice your life gets better. But the one thing you can't choose is the effect negative thoughts have on your mind and body, the illnesses, anxiety and stress you inadvertently inflict on yourself by giving your mind consistently negative instructions through the use of negative words.

With all these techniques, it's important to note that repetition makes a difference. My former client didn't say, "I have phenomenal coping skills" five times and found that her life changed overnight. She used the phrase as an interruptive tool each and every time she felt her mind straying into negative thought patterns. By the time she had improved, she had said the phrase out loud hundreds of times—as well as having it as the screensaver on her phone, written on her mirror, in her car—and it had become true. You repeat negative thoughts in your head all day long, and they become true. The good news is, the repetition of encouraging phrases is just as powerful as the repetition of negative ones, so make sure you give the former a chance to really sink in before you give up on it.

You can just say it but the benefits of writing it and reading it, making it your screen saver, putting it on your phone alerts and changing your computer passwords to say, "I have phenomenal coping skills" give you constantly better results. With that amount of repetition and mental absorption, it will sink in and nourish you like lotion on dry skin.

I truly believe that every single one of us has the ability to get back to that baby in the departure lounge: to have the phenomenal confidence and lack of fear or worry for what's going to come next. You came into the world exactly like that, and I promise you that you don't need to do years of therapy to get it back. You simply need to take responsibility for the words and pictures in your head. Once you do, your life will never be the same.

CHAPTER THREE
Why You Don't Want To Be A Lottery Winner

Once you replace negative thoughts with positive ones, you'll start having positive results.
Willie Nelson, Musician

One of the things you learn as a therapist is that deep down, most people want the same things. They want love, in the form of affirming relationships. They want security, usually in the form of money and social ties. And they desire success, or the feeling that they've made a contribution and accomplished something. But alongside that, you learn something else: that even though most people want these things, they often act in a way that runs counter to attaining them.

How else do you explain people who insist they want to get married, but repeatedly get romantically involved with unavailable, abusive, or non-committal people? Or those who insist they want to be credit card debt free, and then proceed to buy a shiny new watch or car and new clothes at every turn? These actions don't make much logical sense unless you understand another one of the fundamental truths of the human mind. This truth is that when left to its own devices, the mind rejects the unfamiliar and returns to the familiar.

To be honest, this can be a rather frustrating part of being a therapist. You want to see your clients achieve love, success, and money, but they seem to insist on going after the opposite. But like most things, if you go back to our evolutionary origins, it begins to make a bit more sense. After all, when we lived in tribal times, venturing off on our own would be undoubtedly risky. In the absence of the modern conveniences we have today, we were not able to survive on our own as we are now; we needed our immediate tribe to help us procure food, warmth, and connection. Furthermore, the next tribe over could be hostile or harboring dangerous predators we didn't know how to defend ourselves against. Indeed, sticking to the familiar is what kept us alive.

But this penchant for going back to the familiar sticks with us today and causes so many of the problems that send people into my office. I used to see this a lot when I was working on reality TV, especially on weight loss shows. The celebrities I was tasked with helping had been given virtually every resource a person who wants to lose weight could want: trainers, healthy food, chefs, state-of-the-art gyms, mental support, etc. Thanks to all this physical, emotional, and spiritual support, they couldn't help but lose weight. But as soon as they had gained some success, they'd say to me: "All I think about is the moment the show is over so I can celebrate with pizza and ice cream."

In the absence of this knowledge about the mind rejecting the unfamiliar, this seems entirely counterintuitive. They finally had the thing they claimed they wanted so badly—weight loss—and all their mind could fixate on was going back to what was familiar, which was eating an excess of unhealthy foods and gaining weight. On a less public scale, this is precisely why so many diets fail for so many people (something we'll discuss more in Chapter Seven). For people who have long been unhappy with their weight, weight loss is unfamiliar. On the other hand, dieting and then breaking the diet *is* familiar, so this is the dynamic they go back to over and over again.

Eating the same food is familiar, so we don't like taking sugar out of our coffee. But the great news is that after a while, the new taste is familiar and the old sugary coffee becomes unfamiliar and even unpleasant. You do have to stick with it for a while, as the familiar kicks in with repetition—and then you get rewarded.

This logic can be applied to things much more consequential than coffee and tea. Even our familiarity with traditional gender roles shape our behavior. According to research, girls as young as six are less likely to think that members of their own gender can be intellectually brilliant. This has nothing to do with innate ability. Rather, it is a reflection of the way our society and pop culture model lots of men in power—everything from politicians and high-powered executives to superheroes in films—whereas women are usually supporting roles that are merely supplementary to "brilliant" men. Powerful, brilliant men are culturally familiar; powerful, brilliant women are less so.

As researchers found and published in Science, January 2017 edition: "These stereotypes discourage women's pursuit of many prestigious careers—that is, women are underrepresented in fields whose members cherish brilliance (such as physics and philosophy). At age six, girls begin to avoid activities said to be for children who are 'really, really smart.' These findings suggest that gendered notions of brilliance are acquired early and have an immediate effect on children's interests."

In essence, the model of femininity that becomes familiar to six-year-olds is not one of scientists, and inventors, and physicists. Sadly, it means that level of intellectual aspiration becomes unfamiliar to young girls and thus they're less likely to go after it.

We see meta-levels of this dynamic play out frequently in our society. For example, before Barack Obama was elected President, young African Americans did not perceive that it was possible for them to be President one day. Studies showed they didn't even aspire to it. But after two terms of his administration, the idea of a black President has become familiar in the minds of many young African Americans, therefore they increasingly respond that they do want to grow up to be President when surveyed. This is a national-level shift that happened in the space of just a few years.

This may sound like reason to despair. If wealth, success, and love aren't familiar to you because of a family background or history you had no part in choosing, how can you ever overcome this and find happiness for yourself? But there is good news:

We can actively choose to make the familiar things we don't want in our lives, unfamiliar.

In addition, we can choose to make the unfamiliar things we do want, familiar. In fact, studies show repeatedly that our familiarity with certain feelings is not fixed; we are constantly relearning what's familiar. You have to start the behavior—for example, going to the gym or drinking your coffee without sugar—and you must repeat to yourself over and over, "I will make this familiar," and you will.

Feast and famine

One of the other examples where we see this truth play out so predictably is with lottery winners. On the face of it, it would be hard to find someone that doesn't want to win the lottery. It seems like the ideal situation: being able to do whatever you want without having to worry about the cost. But why is it, then, that so many winners end up worse off financially just a few years after hitting the jackpot?

As reported in The Atlantic magazine: "A Camelot survey found that the most popular things Brits spent their winnings on were relatively flashy—properties, cars, and vacations. Similarly, an oft-quoted study of 35,000 lottery winners in Florida found that 1,900 winners filed for bankruptcy within five years—and that while the large infusion of cash reduced the probability of bankruptcy during the first two years of winning, it increased the odds of bankruptcy three to five years out."

The reason for this is that lottery winners are not used to the feeling of being financially carefree. If you've never had money, you don't know what it feels like to invest, to save, or to have spare cash at the end of the month.

What is most familiar to you is getting your pay check, and then spending most of it until you're down to the last few dollars in the days before your new check comes. The feeling of having cash stashed away in the bank is not familiar to you, so you don't do it, even when you have significantly more money.

This is, unfortunately, one of the reasons our society is so unequal. Because wealthy children grow up in families where the trappings of wealth are familiar to them, they are more likely to be predisposed to being wealthy themselves. This isn't because they get an inheritance necessarily (though some do) but because the very concept of wealth and having plenty of money is familiar to them.

Indeed, in my experiences with my clients over the years, I've found that their attitude towards finances and scarcity of money can be one of the hardest things to shift. The reason for that, of course, is that people think they have a problem with money when in reality they have a problem with scarcity. They may have a belief deep down that says, "There will never be enough" or "I don't deserve to have everything I want" or "Everything I have, I eventually lose." They will never ask for a pay rise (even if they deserve it) and they will always struggle to meaningfully save. But the great irony—one that we see in the research about lottery winners described above—is that their problems with money can almost never be solved with more money.

So, how can we change it? I've found my clients have a lot of success by making a fundamental shift in how they think about money and reframing it as something else entirely. You see, we form relationships with money very early on, usually by watching our parents' relationship to it. Then, no matter how much or how little money we go on to earn, that relationship shapes our money beliefs. What would happen if we reframed the thing we have that relationship with entirely. It's not money, it is *energy*. By making a new relationship with a new thing, we can shed our old beliefs and make a new one familiar.

You will find the exercise on the next page very helpful:

For some reason, once we make that switch, those phrases don't sound quite as convincing, do they? Once we make the idea of money as a renewable resource—our personal energy and output—more familiar, we see that money can come and go a lot more easily. It holds less power over us because we see it as a direct result of our own efforts, rather than something that we have to fight and claw for.

This idea of money as a more fluid resource is something that people who have a lot of money tend to live by. They give and receive money easily; they understand that there is a dynamism to money, that coming and going is part of its nature. While sometimes they may have less cash flow, they never necessarily feel "poor." Indeed, just as we can be sure with every exhale an inhale will follow, they are sure that they can receive money just as easily as they get rid of it.

Exercise

The easiest way to see how this can work is to write down all of your self-limiting or long-held beliefs about money. Common phrases that come up are:

I can never make enough money
I can't keep money
Money seems to slip through my fingers
Money doesn't grow on trees, it only comes through graft and strife
I don't deserve more money
I am not worth more money
Spiritual people don't chase money
Me getting more means others getting less

Now, once you've written down those beliefs, switch *money* for *energy*:

I can never make enough energy
I can't keep energy
Energy seems to slip through my fingers
Energy doesn't grow on trees, it only comes through graft and strife
I don't deserve more energy
I am not worth more energy
Spiritual people don't chase energy
There is enough for everyone

Once they know this, they also have less of a problem asking for more remuneration in response to their "energy." They ask for pay rises when they know it feels fair. They put their rates up with their clients, knowing that the right clients will be willing to pay and the ones who aren't a good fit will go elsewhere. They say no to projects that aren't worth their time or effort to make way for larger, more ambitious (and lucrative) projects that are. When they do have a windfall, they don't feel the need to get rid of it in a hurry.

In other words, they make the concept of money (or energy) as a fluid, dynamic resource familiar, and shed the idea that they will never have enough by simply asking for more. You can do that too—not just with money but with everything that causes you pain or hardship.

Choose what to make familiar and unfamiliar

I once had a client who had been in so many failed relationships that she was embarrassed to tell new dating prospects about her romantic past. It didn't make sense—this woman was beautiful, smart, intelligent and entirely financially self-sufficient. But still, over and over she would pursue men who would put her second and not "show up" in a way that demonstrated they really cared.

Meanwhile, this woman would try and win them over and persuade them to stay by being overly attentive, helpful, and eager to please. This would only drive them away further, as they would get irritated by her eagerness and treat her even worse. It was, to be honest, quite sad to watch this happen. After each failed relationship, she would feel so disappointed in herself and would internalize whatever insults the former partner had instilled in her.

I asked this client, as is my normal practice, to describe her relationship with her father. He was a very unhappy man, often came home drunk in the afternoon, and would promptly take over the house, making demands of her mother, often flying into fits of rage. He'd say disparaging things to my client and routinely diminish her if she wasn't absolutely perfect. The next morning after these drunken fits, he would merely pretend that nothing had happened, and eat breakfast as if everything was okay again. She had learned, over the years, to ride out his scary episodes in the hope of everything returning to normal in the morning. This cycle of emotional peaks and valleys became very familiar to her.

Upon learning this history, I said to my client: "Your father used to put you down, diminish your feelings, ignore you when he was drunk—but then everything would be okay the next day if you didn't cause a fuss. And guess what? Now you choose the guy who makes you feel similarly." She promptly realized that this was true.

Her friends often can't see what attracts her to these less-than-desirable men, and often remark that they are unable to see any redeeming qualities. But, of course, my client was not so much going after his personality, as the pattern he represented. She had often heard herself say, "I feel like I've known him my whole life", upon meeting a new guy. Because, of course, she kind of had. She was falling for the familiar, even though the familiar was a terrible choice for her. Not only does the mind want to return to what is familiar it also likes us to recreate scenarios that remind us of our childhood but to put a happy ending on it. Hence going for men like her father but trying to make them love and respect her in a way he never did. Life is far too short to keep trying to change the ending. We need to change the beginning, so instead of finding someone cold and trying to make them kind, start with someone kind—it makes life so much easier.

This client needed to make being praised, appreciated and being in a mutually equal relationship familiar—rather than feeling as though she was walking on eggshells, waiting for someone's temper tantrum to pass so she could mend things once again. She told me when she met men who seemed to respect her and be emotionally stable, she would immediately feel they were "too good" for her and she found she wasn't attracted to their even-keeled personalities. I told her to replace that dialogue with the phrase: "No one is too good for me; I will make being loved and respected familiar." Once she had spotted the pattern in the men she had historically gone for (ones that reminded her of her father) she immediately turned the other way when she saw hints of that pattern arise. She had developed a strong aversion to the familiar (to turn away from it) because she now knew it was harming her. Alongside that, she developed a strong attraction to the empowering and praising types of men that make good partners.

But there was one other thing my client had to make familiar in order to receive it from the men she was dating: praise. As a child, she had only ever heard criticism from her father, and virtually nothing from her subservient mother. She had never experienced what it was like to be praised for her personality or innate qualities—only for her actions to please her father—so she didn't go after guys who praised her simply for being herself. In order to make praise familiar, however, she couldn't look outward; she had to start with herself. I gave her a script to run through every morning while doing her hair in the mirror. She would repeat out loud the self-praising affirmations that no one else in her life had ever told her, "I'm a wonderful, caring partner," "I am attractive and lovable," "I easily attract and maintain lasting love and respect."

While these phrases might sound arrogant, they are not. The point here is not to run around and proclaim your greatness to the barista or your colleagues; the point is to familiarize the sound of praise to *yourself*. The more you repeat this, the more you'll believe it, and you'll soon find that you are not attracted to people who don't also praise you. You have made praise familiar.

I've worked with so many highly successful people and one thing I notice about them is that they are very willing to tell you out loud, without hesitation, what they are good at. This is because praise and self-confidence are so familiar to them that they don't find it uncomfortable to say out loud what they excel at. Whether that confidence comes from having a perfect childhood with encouraging parents or from the inner work they've done on themselves in spite of a rotten childhood doesn't matter—anyone can choose to make praise familiar. And indeed, once you do, you'll find it is the greatest gift you can give yourself. Present praise to yourself, make it familiar and then your mind will present it back. Very soon, praise will stop being what you do and become who you are.

Start small and familiarize pleasure

There are probably areas of your life that you'd like to make unfamiliar. They don't have to be as consequential as choosing a life partner though. Here's an example: One of my clients would always order a burger and fries because it cost $8 whereas a salad cost $12 and she resented that extra cost. And then she learned to make spending more money on healthy foods familiar and putting junk into her body unfamiliar. She realized that spending more on good food was actually cost effective because she was spending less on medication, weight loss books, and pills.

If lounging around after work and playing on your iPad is familiar to you, make getting off the train or bus a stop early and walking the rest of the way while listening to your iPad familiar instead. If sleeping in until the last possible second and being late to work is familiar to you, set yourself a challenge to get into work five minutes early every day for a week. All of sudden the different train times and routine will become familiar, and you won't have to force yourself to do it any longer.

Pick one thing that you're going to stick to for a week—you can start small if that's more comfortable—no sugar in your coffee or eating an apple every mid-morning instead of your usual unhealthy snack. Praise yourself every day in the place of self-criticism. Pay attention to how it becomes slightly easier with each passing day. Then, you can start thinking about applying what you've learned from making this small unfamiliar task familiar to a much larger idea: your self-worth, career potential, or relationship.

Once you know that it's possible to make the familiar unfamiliar and vice versa, you can go with confidence in the direction of your dreams.

Making shame and hurt unfamiliar

One of the common issues I've dealt with as a therapist is clients from religious backgrounds who can't seem to shake some of the habits of shame that were instilled in them from a very young age. While religion can certainly be a positive force for good in the world it can, unfortunately, mutate and leave some people with incredible shame and hurt when their family or religious leader has dubbed them as someone who doesn't "measure up."

It's so disheartening to see individuals whose families have alienated them because they no longer subscribe to the socio-cultural norms of a given religion, and it's unfortunately very common. But the good news is, these limiting belief systems are not embedded or innate— they are learned.

Religious or not, many people have familiar beliefs instilled by family that are no longer useful to them. Whether it's "I'm not a good son" or "I ruined my honor by having sex before marriage," these beliefs only have power over you *because* they are so familiar. You may think your only options for ridding yourself of these beliefs are years of therapy or a magical ability to go back in time and reclaim your childhood. But there's another, much less time-consuming way.

If your habitual shame dates back to childhood, it is very likely that it is not *your* shame. It is likely that your mother or father or grandparents instilled in you their own sense of shame about not measuring up, and then made it so familiar to you that you feel as though it is yours. It is an unfortunate fact that it's possible for us to learn shame. Just as you can make a cat or dog feel shameful if you yell at it each time it jumps on the couch, you can make a human feel shame if they don't live up to some culturally imposed standard which you remind them of constantly.

But you don't have to live with it.

Try the next exercise:

Exercise

Start saying out loud to yourself:

This is not my shame
It doesn't belong to me
I can let it go

Imagine it into a large heavy case and handing it back to the person who gave it to you and the relief as you no longer have to carry that weight with you.

In other words, hand it back to the person that gave it to you. They don't have to know you've done that, but the image of you handing back your shame to the person who imposed it on you is deeply liberating.

Once you've handed back, it's no longer yours and therefore no longer familiar to you. Now you can make new positive beliefs familiar:

For example:

I am a good son
I have inherent value no matter what church I go to
No one can make me feel inferior

These new beliefs will, if repeated, replace the spiral of shame you've lived in for so long.

As you look forward in your life, you are bound to encounter situations that can cause you hurt or anger. To avoid this hurt or anger mutating into shame or unhelpful belief systems, you have to make sure you express your feelings as close to a triggering event occurring as possible. While it isn't always advisable or possible to express your hurt or anger to the person that caused it, you always have the option of going somewhere private and expressing your hurt out loud. For instance, if your boss or a relative has upset you, you can shut yourself in the toilet and run the taps or flush the toilet to muffle the sound while you say out loud "I am hurt that my boss is taking credit for my work. I am hurt that my brother-in-law always criticizes me."

If you say: "I am hurt by my sister's unwillingness to call me back" and then follow it with: "I am loveable and that cannot be diminished by my sister's behavior," you avoid creating those old unhelpful beliefs and you recognize that someone else's behavior cannot make you feel bad about yourself unless you allow it to and you have the power to not allow that.

One thing I noticed very early in my career is that people who are happy and balanced express their hurt easily. It's not hard to do, you simply have to get used to saying, "You hurt my feelings when ……". The most effective way is to start with praise: "I love you, you're my best friend/sister/daughter, etc., but I was hurt when you forgot my birthday. I don't want to hold onto it so I'm just expressing it to you so I can let it go."

Expressing your hurt as close to the event as possible is for your benefit, so you don't hold onto the feelings and let them fester. When you can't say it out loud because the person that hurt you is your boss or a difficult relative you can still say it in private when you are alone or driving your car. Saying out loud, just to yourself, "I was hurt by …… it hurt me when …….", is so effective at getting the hurt out and the more you do it the easier it becomes.

What's wrong with you and everyone else, too?

As well as observing my three categories of clients I also observed that all my clients only ever have three categories of problems or three things that were wrong with them. Identifying the three things wrong with you and with everyone else, too gives you an insight and understanding of what is influencing and affecting the people around you and helps you to deal with their behaviors with an insight that benefits everyone. I talked in earlier chapters about how my clients have a presenting problem but the real issue that needs addressing is what lies beneath. What lies beneath any client's presenting problem will always be one of these three beliefs:

I am not enough. I am covering this in detail in Chapter Eight.

I want something but it's not available to me. So many clients consult with me desperate and longing to be free of their issues but alongside the issues, which include depression, alcoholism, obesity and lack of success, is a fixed belief: "I want to be free of depression but I have the depressed gene just like my mum/ I am desperate to stop drinking but I come from a family of alcoholics/ I want to acquire wealth but I don't have a college degree. My family are all manual workers so I don't think it's possible/ I want to be confident but I was born shy/ no one can have it all/ I want to speak on stage but I am crippled by anxiety." The fixed beliefs my clients hold about themselves are the biggest blocks to achieving their goals. You no doubt have some fixed beliefs, too and it's very useful to ask yourself: "Why do I believe that? Where did that belief come from? Who gave it to me? Who gave it to them? Why am I still believing it all these years later." The point of doing this is that the minute you begin to question a belief you no longer hold it to be true, because as you question you chip away at it until it's gone. Many people who have dazzling success were not born to a position where it was made available to them—quite the opposite. Oprah Winfrey, Barack Obama, Meghan Markle all found success—it did not find them. Everything is available to you and the first step to achieving that is to fix that new belief firmly in your mind in place of the old one.

I am different so I can't connect (so it's hard for me to have love because I am different). The third problem that so many of my clients present with is a powerful belief they are different. You can see how this looping thought works. The common denominator of all our emotional issues is that we feel that we are not enough and we feel different so we can't connect. Yet our survival is linked to our need to connect so it becomes a spiral, a vicious circle. Since our greatest fear is to be different, the very fact that you think you are different means you are the same as everyone and they are the same as you. It's coded into our genes to be the same as everyone else, rather than to stand out because that could have threatened our survival. Today it is good to be outstanding and it doesn't threaten your survival.

Here is a question for you: Why do you feel different?

Below are the common answers:

· No personality, I'm too short, too fat, too thin, not educated, not interesting, not talented, not attractive.

· I don't have enough money, praise, love, success.

· I am not enough, I am not valued, I have never felt as though I mattered or was important.

Even millionaires, models and superstars feel these same feelings.

My happiest clients don't have any of these beliefs. They, in fact, have the opposite beliefs: "I am enough; I am here with something valuable to offer; love happiness and success are available to me; I connect with people easily because I belong to life and I am always supported by the universe."

You can have these beliefs, too simply by using the methods in this book to make them a part of who you are instead of something you make yourself do from time to time.

CHAPTER FOUR
To Be Successful, Do This First

If you do what you have always done, you get what you have always got.
Mark Twain, Author

As I wrote in the Introduction, part of my reason for writing this book was to share with my readers the commonalities I've observed in all of my happiest, most successful clients—the clients who "have it all." Often, when we look at successful people, we assume they have a whole raft of superior abilities and privileges that aren't attainable for us. The truth is they don't. They've just learned how to make their mind work for them, rather than against them. My goal is to teach you the same.

Another common assumption about successful people is that they don't have any problems. That they are immune to the personal, relational, and professional problems that seem to afflict most people. Some even believe that successful people are immune from boredom and life's mundanity! This couldn't be further from the truth. In fact, the highly successful rock stars, CEOs, and leaders that have sat in my therapy chair tend to have far more complicated problems due to their high profiles and complex lives. Contrary to popular belief, money, fame, and success do not exempt you from life's annoyances.

Despite all this, my successful clients seem to share a common trait when it comes to tackling their problems and going after their dreams. Each morning, when they get up, they do what they hate or dislike and get it done first. Indeed, doing what you hate—and getting it out of the way by doing it first—is one of the quickest ways to inject success into your life. If you can create this habit and apply it across your life, you will see your life change.

I'll start by giving you an example:

A celebrity client I worked with in Los Angeles was so overweight that his doctors warned he needed to lose a staggering half of his body weight in order to reclaim his normal health. He was on the fast track to a whole host of illnesses including heart disease, stroke, and diabetes if he did not quickly begin a weight loss regimen and stick to it. Despite these dire warnings, this client insisted that he had an absolute hatred of all forms of exercise. He felt sweaty and nervous at the mere thought of going to the gym. His response was to put it off all day, which only meant his self-loathing would grow and grow until he finally gave up on the idea of going to the gym altogether. Feeling guilty and like a loser, he would end the night eating fried chicken and pizza, feeling like a failure and feeling remorseful and depressed.

This client appealed for my help in reversing his hatred of exercise. He wanted a magic wand, but instead, I gave him a simple prescription. I told him he was to get up at 5 am every day before it was light outside and before he had time to eat anything and go for a brisk walk around his Beverly Hills neighborhood for thirty minutes. He was aghast, saying "Marisa—I thought you were going to make this easier for me, not torture me!" I insisted that if he committed to doing this for just one week, I would do it with him, and that it would become immeasurably easier by the end of the week. If it didn't, I promised we'd try another tactic.

There were several reasons I did this. At this point, my client could barely run, let alone go to a gym, so I knew that I had to give him a regime that allowed for as few excuses as possible. If all he had to do was walk around the block, he couldn't complain that the gym equipment didn't work for his size. At that early hour of the morning, he couldn't complain that the neighbors would stare at his weight, as they wouldn't be awake yet to make him feel embarrassed. He couldn't say his stomach was too full of food because he would not have time to eat beforehand. And, most importantly, he wouldn't have the entire day to fill his head with negative thoughts of how far he had to go in his weight loss and talk himself out of exercising.

The first few days, I nearly had to pry him out of bed and into his running shoes. As we walked out of the house and into the darkness, he had so many excuses for why this was a bad idea. I simply dismissed every one and told him he had promised to give me seven days. Each and every day, when we got back from the brisk walk, he remarked: "Oh that wasn't so bad" and went about his day. But something else crucial happened: He found himself more willing to stick to his healthy food regime and less keen to binge on the fast food and sugary snacks that were normally so tempting to him. Because he had done what he hates and, crucially, he had done it first, he was set up for success for the rest of the day and was less willing to sabotage his efforts. In just seven days, this simple trick—doing what you hate, and doing it first—had taken his weight loss effort from an impossible task to a manageable journey and he went on to lose half his body weight.

When you do what you hate, you might just start to like it

For some people, this idea can be confusing. When they hear that successful people do what they don't like first in order to get to where they need to be, they sometimes say: "But Marisa, I thought you teach the idea that we should learn to love every aspect of our life by telling our mind that we love the things we don't."

It is still true that everything I advised in Chapters One and Two are vital to your success. You must latch on to the belief that your mind does what it thinks you want it to do, and that the words and pictures you use repeatedly are very powerful in creating how you actually feel. However, at the same time, I'm not here to espouse a Pollyanna version of the universe—it wouldn't be particularly helpful if I did. Life will always come with adversity, drudgery, and things you don't enjoy. If it didn't, then the most wonderful moments of life would seem dull and unremarkable. We need a bit of pain and discomfort in order to experience true joy, but what we *don't* have to do is allow that pain and discomfort to run (and potentially ruin) our lives.

The rule of this chapter is about learning how to meet the things that cause you annoyance, discomfort, or pain and then lessening their power over you by getting them out of the way and doing them first. This can be boring things such as admin, doing your accounts, or following up on payments owed to you. Or it can be

I Am Enough

more consequential things such as confronting an abusive colleague or telling a family member you need to take a break from speaking with them or breaking up with a partner. In a sense, there will always be things in your life that you don't like doing, and you have two options for how to deal with them. You can say: "I don't like this, but I'm going to do it now and feel good about it all day" or you can say: "I don't want to do this so I'm going to put it off and torture myself all day." If you choose the latter, this can often mean you end up putting off these decisions for weeks, months, and even years, thereby ruining your life in the process. It is coded into our genes to run away from fear. This was very useful when you were running away from a predator but today, instead, we run from a task that we do not want to do, especially if we feel nervous or fear failing at that task. We translate the resistance to an assignment as fear and we run away from it. This is easily overcome using the exercises within.

It doesn't matter what it is: Getting the thing you hate doing out of the way by prioritizing it has the power to change your life. I realized that when I went back to visit the overweight celebrity client of mine. He was so proud that he had continued in his weight loss effort. I asked him what had helped him the most, and he said that establishing the habit of his exercise regime first thing in the morning had been especially helpful. He said all along he'd been waiting for the motivation to exercise to appear, and would spend each day watching the hours go by and his drive to exercise diminish with each passing minute. But interestingly, only when he *began* exercising, did he feel any motivation to continue doing it.

By the time of my follow up visit, he had graduated from his walk around the neighborhood to go to a local gym, and he even remarked that he'd begun to *enjoy* his daily visits. This demonstrates one of the most unexpected side effects of the do-what-you-hate-first strategy: when you do what you hate, you might just start to like it.

Whether it's dealing with your colleagues with clear communication and boundaries, doing your taxes, or going for a jog, the reason we sometimes grow to love what we hate is based on science. In New York Times journalist Charles Duhigg's best-selling book, "The

Power of Habit," which is all about the science behind the habits we stick to, he wrote: "All habits—no matter how large or small—have three components, according to neurological studies. There's a cue—a trigger for a particular behavior; a routine, which is the behavior itself; and a reward, which is how your brain decides whether to remember a habit for the future."

In his book, Duhigg recounts the history of toothpaste as an invention to underline the strength of this theory. Prior to the invention of Pepsodent in the early 1900s, few people brushed their teeth in America. Then advertising executive Claude C. Hopkins got his hands on a new invention: Pepsodent toothpaste, and he decided to go about finding a way to sell it to Americans. He first thought he could market it based on the idea that it rid your teeth of "film" or the plaque that builds up when you don't brush. But when sales spiked, market research found that something different was at play:

"When researchers at competing companies started interviewing customers, they found that people said that if they forgot to use Pepsodent, they realized their mistake because they missed that cool, tingling sensation in their mouths," Duhigg wrote. "They expected—they craved—that slight irritation. If it wasn't there, their mouths didn't feel clean. Claude Hopkins, it turns out, wasn't selling beautiful teeth. He was selling a sensation. Once people craved that cool tingling—once they equated it with cleanliness—brushing became a habit."

The fact that a minty flavor was added to toothpaste at all was an accident. It wasn't meant to leave users feeling minty fresh, but rather, help the product last longer on the shelves. But brushers came to look forward to the feeling of the minty tingling that came after they brushed, and so they created a habit they once hadn't even thought of and probably could never be convinced to do otherwise—just as my client had grown accustomed to the feeling of accomplishment he got from his early morning workouts.

While this tooth-brushing example is a great illustration of how new habits can be formed in a positive sense, the same science applies to a litany of bad habits, too. As Duhigg goes on to write: "This, scientists say, is how habits emerge, and why they are so powerful:

They create neurological cravings. Most of the time, these cravings emerge so gradually that we're not really aware they exist. But as our brains start to associate certain cues (a chocolate bar!) with certain rewards (yummy and it melts in my mouth!), a subconscious craving emerges. And so, whenever we see chocolate bars or chocolate cookies in the break room we start craving them —even if, just moments before, we weren't hungry at all."

Remember what Duhigg said about the science behind habits? It involves a cue, a behavior, and a reward. If you want to create a new habit of doing what you hate first, then you need to focus on the reward system associated. Let's take a look at the celebrity weight loss client again. In order to establish his new habit, I gave him a cue: the alarm clock. Each and every time it went off, he had to drag himself out of bed, no questions, justifications, or excuses. The behavior itself was the jog or walk around the block. And then the reward was the feeling of accomplishment and lack of guilt he maximized all day long by getting the jog over with first thing. Once he grew to love the feeling of not descending further into self-loathing with each passing hour, he didn't want to go back to not exercising. In effect, he didn't grow to love the behavior, but the reward itself.

This can be applied to virtually anything. Want to eat healthier but hate cooking? Start your week by prepping healthy meals on Sunday nights—doing what you hate first—and focus on how easy it is when you get home from work to quickly heat up a healthy, satisfying dinner. If you're tired of being underpaid by your clients, start your week by politely sending out a notice that you are raising your rates and reap the reward you get from the feeling that you're honoring your talents and abilities. If you are tired of being single but hate putting yourself out there, set yourself a challenge to talk to one stranger in the first half of each day or set up one online dating date each weekend. Soon, you'll find you begin to love these spontaneous interactions.

When I was first starting out as a therapist and a writer, I knew I had to put myself out there. I knew that my techniques and methods had the power to change people's lives, and I wanted journalists and magazines to write about me and my methods so I could reach more people and get an agent to sell my books. However, the thought of picking up the phone and "pitching" myself to busy journalists and editors was not appealing as it involved rejection (which is, of course, our greatest fear). There were so many things I'd rather do instead, but I knew I had to prioritize it or my ideas and book manuscripts would sit in drawers literally and metaphorically unless I made a concerted effort to raise my public profile. I set myself the challenge of calling one journalist, editor, or publication each and every day before I did anything else (in the days before email, calling was the way).

I devoted 15 minutes a day to this practice for weeks and racked up lots of rejections in the process. However, I knew rejection is incredibly common for writers—Harry Potter's author J.K. Rowling's first book was rejected by several publishers before it went on to sell hundreds of millions—so I knew persistence was vital. When I called one magazine after seeing an article they'd written about using the power of the mind to walk across hot coals, they commissioned me to write an article about the power that hypnosis has to influence the body. After that, they loved it so much they asked me to write a regular column, which led to many other columns and, eventually, coverage in all of Britain's and many of America's major magazines and many other international publications.

It all seems so easy now, but I know this would never have happened had I not set myself a goal to do the thing I hated every day. By the time I had raised my public profile, I had become very comfortable at pitching and making cold calls; as we know, the mind learns from repetition, and I'd repeated the scary activity so many times it had ceased to intimidate me. Of course, the irony now was that my public profile as a writer and therapist had become so widespread that most of the interest from journalists now came to me!

Drawing on the lessons from the first two chapters, it's really important for you to change your internal dialogue to convince yourself that you are "choosing" to do what you hate. The first week, it certainly won't feel like that. You will feel like my client being dragged out of bed at 5 am each morning about to do something he detests. But if you interrupt your mind and change your language to something more neutral: "I am choosing to do this first, for the feeling of the reward I get," you make it far more manageable. Other phrases that can work are: "I am determined to be successful, therefore I do what I don't want to do and I do it first" as well as: "I'm choosing to do what I don't want to do. I'm choosing to feel great about doing what I don't want to do. I'm choosing to do it first," reminding yourself that successful people do what they hate first and if you want the same success you must choose to do the same.

This practice is very much a self-reinforcing one. That is, the more you repeat these phrases above, the more your mind will believe them (even if it feels futile or unconvincing at first). The more you believe them, the more you will do the thing you hate and do it first. And then, the more you do the thing you hate, the more motivation you will find you have to continue. My favorite saying that I repeat a lot is, first you make your habits—and then your habits make you. Make your habits positive by doing what you dislike first and then your habits will make you more successful.

If you're still unconvinced that doing what you hate (and doing it first) is the key to success, I want to point out a metaphor that I believe is so helpful when thinking about doing the things we hate. If you think about every author, artist, athlete, or successful entrepreneur you admire, I can almost guarantee that they have a high tolerance for doing the thing they hate.

Think of it like this: If there was a success club and you really wanted to become a member—you *really* wanted to belong to a group where everyone else was successful and you felt you belonged there too—would you pay the membership fee? What if I told you there was no fee but in order to be a member you had to commit to doing what you did not want to do. You had to do the activities you disliked first. Would you do it? I think you would. So start now and anytime you have resistance remind yourself that "doing what I don't want to do first is how I get membership to the success club." Then it becomes more appealing as you are focusing on your reward.

I've worked with clients from virtually every discipline and industry—people who have their so-called "dream jobs"—and every single one of them has to do things they hate from time to time. If you're an entrepreneur, you'll have to deal with uncertainty, risk, and early morning phone calls; if you're an athlete, you'll have to train each and every morning even if you don't feel like it; if you're a writer, you'll have to work alone, send pitches and put yourself out there. You can't have the glory and the accolades of these professions without the unpleasant bits. But what you *can* do is prioritize the parts you least like so that it doesn't take over your life. In other words, when you get up in the morning, do your disliked tasks first. You'll be glad for the rest of the day that you did—and you'll be able to enjoy the parts of your life and career that you do like.

The Three Ps

To close this chapter, I want to answer a question I once got from a client, that stuck with me. After outlining this strategy for her, she remarked that she had begun doing the things she hates first, and that it was taking up nearly half her day. "It's only after lunchtime that I begin to start doing things that I don't hate," she wrote. "Is this normal?"

I want to be clear that this method should not feel as though it's taking over your life. While life certainly has plenty of less enjoyable bits, the feeling of "hate" probably doesn't apply to that many of them. I don't want to sound like I'm espousing the idea that you should fill your hours with things you don't enjoy in order to be successful. To the contrary.

If you hate every waking hour of your job, that's a good reason to look at the structure of your life and work and reconsider your career path. If you hate spending time with your partner, it's possible that you are not in the right relationship. If studying for law school gives you great insecurity that you might be making the wrong choice by being a lawyer, I don't want you to override that feeling. If talking to your colleagues or boss makes you feel abused or disrespected, I don't want you to do that first—I don't want you to do it at all!

If you're having trouble delineating between doing something you hate (that will take you to where you want to go) and doing something that is broadly not serving you, it can be helpful to use the "Three Ps" test. Ask yourself is this thing: Permanent? Personal? Pervasive?

If something is not permanent, you can usually get through it if it's in service of what you want. If it's a project at work or writing a proposal, learning something new or cleaning up your finances—those things will all, eventually, go away. But if it's your career path, your choice in partner, or being in over your head with a mortgage, those are more lasting. You can get through anything with enough perseverance, but just make sure what you're trying to get through actually has an endpoint.

Asking yourself, "Is it personal?" means figuring out if it's something that you alone can fix. Be it a bad attitude, habit, or belief system. It's always possible to fix things that are personal because you are in charge. However, if you're being mistreated or abused by another person, that is a dynamic you should not necessarily power through, as it isn't entirely in your control. I wouldn't want you to do something you hate first if it means letting someone mistreat you.

Lastly, is it pervasive? The things that you hate which can lead you to success are usually annoyances and preferences rather than structural life issues. If what you hate seems to creep into every facet of your life, you shouldn't prioritize it. You should change it!

I hope this helps you see the difference between prioritizing the small tasks in life that you put off and going against your instincts and integrity about what makes you feel good. In other words, doing what you hate and doing it first shouldn't be exhausting and debilitating but, rather, energizing. It should make you enjoy the rest of the hours in your day much more and give you the feeling of accomplishment that leads to you wanting even more accomplishment. Most importantly, it should move you towards the things in life you really want, not away from them.

You can also use PPP to deal with stress. Let's imagine your boss is difficult, your teenager is confrontational or your commute is stressful. Ask yourself is this permanent, personal and all-pervasive? Your boss being difficult is not permanent, as you won't work with him forever. It's not personal, as he is like that with everyone. And it's not all-pervasive, as when you are at home having a lovely dinner or a relaxing bath he is not there.

If it is not PPP all the time, it can't hurt you unless you let it.

CHAPTER FIVE
There Are No Shortcuts - But There Is One Guarantee

Faith is taking the first step even when you don't see the whole staircase.
Martin Luther King Jr, Spokesperson and Leader

You may have noticed that the previous chapter was slightly different to the three that came before it. In the first three chapters, I focused on habits of thought. As a quick review here, those were: Telling your mind exactly what you want it to do, complete with up-to-date and relevant language; taking responsibility for the words and pictures in your head; and making the familiar unfamiliar and vice versa. Then, in Chapter Four, I subtly shifted to focus on a habit of *action* and I gave you a specific action to take every day. This chapter will also focus on a habit of action to integrate into your life.

One of the guiding principles of my methods is the power of repetition. If you repeat anything often enough, whether it's good or bad, you can instill it in your brain. Most people, unaware of this power, repeat negative or unhelpful things, whether that's critical self-talk, bad eating habits, or comparing themselves to others. Each day, as they do those things, they don't see the effect that repetition is unwittingly having on their lives. But the good news is that the flip-side is true, too. The power of repetition can unknowingly work in your favor—provided you repeat the right actions in your daily life.

That is why the next habit of action is so essential:

Do one thing each day in the direction of your dreams.

This may seem incredibly simplistic and obvious to you, but the reality is that it's often overlooked or not executed properly. So often I have clients who work incredibly hard Monday to Friday, hit the weekend with burnout, and then still feel guilty that they are not working on Saturday and Sunday. They often lose sight of what they are working for, in fact. Most of the time, they are miserable, too.

I'm not advising you to work seven days a week flat out. What I am asking you to do is choose one thing in your life that's really important for you to achieve—in any area of your life—and commit to doing one small thing *every day* in service of that, even if it's for just a few minutes. This can be in service of your career, your creative dream, your mental health, or your physical health; the point is to remove the question of "Will I or won't I do it?" from your mind. Once you do that, and begin doing one small thing a day, you will see how powerful the practice of habit and repetition really is.

I've said before in this book that when you do the things that very successful people do, you unknowingly become more and more like them. This is very true when it comes to this habit of action. You see, similar to starting the day by getting your least favorite task out of the way first, committing to a small task every day in service of your dreams of success makes you feel like a winner. Once you feel that way, you begin to act differently. You begin to take on the air of a successful person and believe that you *are* successful. This can have an effect on how other people treat you, how you treat yourself, and what you attract into your life. For instance, at the weekend just do a little work on your website, return a few calls or watch a short training video.

It may seem like a small step, but it's in service of a much bigger goal.

Everyone wants a shortcut

Since I've spent so much time working with all kinds of people, I always get asked: "What makes a successful person stick to their goals?" The answer is that there is no single shortcut to this. We live in a culture that's obsessed with life hacks and quick fixes, but when it comes to the path to success, there really isn't one outward trick. However, in place of that, there is a kind of guarantee: If you show up to something, each and every day, you're guaranteed to get closer to it. If you don't, you won't.

I've worked with a lot of Olympic athletes and they always serve as such a good role model of this. Viewers at home see the moments of glory as they compete and win medals. The athletes, meanwhile, see only the years of pain and sacrifice it took to get there. As Olympic swimmer, Matt Biondi, is quoted as saying: "Persistence can change failure into extraordinary achievement." The same is true for you.

A great example of the power of consistency is what usually happens around Christmas and the holidays. We can enter the month with a solid workout or health routine and say, "I'm just going to take four days off." And then, all of a sudden, it's mid-January and we haven't been to the gym in three weeks. If you allow yourself to remove the guarantee of "showing up," the habit very often falls apart and ceases to be important to you. But when you take action every day—even if it means just going for a brisk walk or doing some stretches on Christmas Day, for example—you continue to move closer to it with ease. Once again, there is no shortcut here, but there is a guarantee: Show up and you'll see results.

That guarantee is why I'm using this chapter to emphasize the power of merely showing up to do the same thing for ten minutes a day. As you move closer to your goal, your goal will begin moving closer to you. This is all based on the law and science of attraction. As Deepak Chopra wrote, "This law states that the whole situation around you is you. 'I am what I see. What I see is me.' Once you see it is only you reflecting yourself back, what happens? You become more self-aware. As self-awareness expands, you become much clearer and focused on what you truly want. Then and only then can the law of attraction work for you reliably."

Doing one thing every day, without fail, in service of who or what you want to be is a guaranteed way to improve the reflection you see of yourself. Once you do that, everything improves, as you begin to believe in yourself and your own capabilities. Then it becomes far easier to move towards everything in life that you want.

It's not too good to be true

"But Marisa, can just five or ten minutes a day doing something *really* make me successful?" I can hear your doubts from here. The answer is yes, it can. It's not too good to be true because the effect of this practice multiplies across your life and, more importantly, your attitude towards your life. When you feel better about yourself you start to conduct yourself with the air of someone who is successful—which in turn makes you successful. It doesn't matter how big or small the daily action is, what matters is that you're beginning to *act like a winner*.

You should really begin to think of your mind as a goal-seeking laser. Just as it listens to the words and pictures you tell yourself to inform how it thinks, it also loves to have concrete goals to work towards. The more specific you can make these, the better. So, it's not "I want to be successful" but rather: "By next year, I want to have written a book draft" or "I want to lose 100 pounds" but rather "I want to commit to cooking more healthy foods during the work week."

Your mind is incredibly pliable as an organism. You may think: "Well, I'm not the kind of person who can stick to anything; I always give up." But that's a story you're telling yourself. If you go to the finish line of any marathon and ask the runners if they've always loved running, a stunning number of them will insist NO! They went from couch potatoes to marathon runners because they began to form a habit of action that they showed up for. They changed their minds about who they are—and you can do the same. It just requires being specific and relentlessly showing up.

I will say, though, that when you're first getting started in establishing this habit of action, you should think carefully about what the one thing you're going to start with might be. It doesn't have to be an extreme commitment. Too often, I see people take on overly-ambitious goals and set themselves up for failure. Just as with the weight loss client in the last chapter, I didn't instruct him to run a 10K every morning; I told him to simply walk around his neighborhood every day. Once he did that, the motivation to do more began to appear. It's one of my favorite sayings because it's so true: Movement manifests motivation.

I also don't want this to be something you hate. The previous chapter's advice and this chapter are separate. The previous chapter was about getting what you dislike done first; this chapter is about *choosing* to commit to something that is going to make you feel like a winner and move you towards your goals. In the best-case scenario, I want you to choose to do something every day that takes you closer to your goal, be it writing, meditation, exercise or working on your business plan. For instance, when I decided to do what I hated, by calling journalists and asking them to write about me, I also decided to make one call every single day even on a Sunday. News desks are open on Sundays and making a call every single day wired that action into me. Instead of dreading it I got it out of the way and felt good because I was taking action every day in the direction of my goals.

Another way to set yourself up for success with your new habit is to have an accountability mechanism. This can really help people stick to a goal. Tell your family or partners (so long as they're supportive of you) about your new goal and ask them to encourage you. Join a social media group of like-minded people sharing their goals or set up a workout buddy you can text with once a day. All of these will increase your chances of sticking to your new goal.

So, whether it's a career goal, a self-care goal, or a personal, spiritual, or creative goal, pick one thing you're going to commit to doing every day for the next few months. Believe in it and enjoy watching the consistency play out in your life in beautiful and unexpected ways. And remember —what you want, wants you. What you are moving towards is moving towards you.

You just have to take the first step.

CHAPTER SIX
Your Mind Is Like A Classroom Of Three-Year-Olds

The ability to delay gratification has implications not only for a person's life, but also for a community, for a people, for a country.
Joachim de Posada, Author

Tell me if this sounds familiar: You stumble into your house after a long day of work, weary due to the day behind you but fully aware it's not over yet. You survey a kitchen that needs cleaning, kids' permission slips that need to be signed, and the email inbox that needs to be cleared. But, you're also desperate to watch the latest episode of the newest show you have recorded. And the chocolate in the cupboard and the wine in your fridge are calling your name—"Just take a break first," they say "then you can finish your 'to do' list."

What do you do first?

This chapter is all about the habit of action that successful people use to respond to that scenario—delaying gratification—as well as the added mind trick that can make that habit stick, which is savoring the reward. I'm going to explain why you won't find success with the former without emphasizing the latter. But first, let's look into the science behind delayed gratification.

You've probably heard of the famous Stanford marshmallow experiment, the premise of which was quite simple. Researchers, led by psychologist Walter Mischel, Ph.D., left preschoolers with a marshmallow and offered them a choice: They could have that one now, or, if they waited until the researcher came back, they could have two. In other words, they asked them to delay a gratification for an increased reward.

The results were striking. According to the American Psychological Association, researchers: "found that teenagers who had waited longer for the marshmallows as preschoolers were more likely to score higher on the SAT, and their parents were more likely to rate them as having a greater ability to plan, handle stress, respond to reason, exhibit self-control in frustrating situations and concentrate without becoming distracted." Mischel went back yet again to revisit the study with participants now in their forties and found that "their willpower differences had largely held up over four decades."

In my years as a therapist, I've definitely observed that people who can delay gratification are more likely to fall in that rare, third category of clients who "have it all." They're the people who know that good things don't happen overnight, that the most lasting satisfaction takes time and effort to wait for, and that it is in the *earning* of things that we feel the most pleasure. This is what fuels successful and driven people to work hard, persevere, and never give up even when things get hard.

Mischel and his fellow researchers went on to provide a framework for how different humans view gratification. As the APA wrote: "He proposed what he calls a 'hot-and-cool' system to explain why willpower succeeds or fails. The cool system is cognitive in nature. It's essentially a thinking system, incorporating knowledge about sensations, feelings, actions, and goals —reminding yourself, for instance, why you shouldn't eat the marshmallow. While the cool system is reflective, the hot system is impulsive and emotional. The hot system is responsible for quick, reflexive responses to certain triggers—such as popping the marshmallow into your mouth without considering the long-term implications. If this framework were a cartoon, the cool system would be the angel on your shoulder and the hot system, the devil. When willpower fails, exposure to a 'hot' stimulus essentially overrides the cool system, leading to impulsive actions. Some people, it seems, may be more or less susceptible to hot triggers. And that susceptibility to emotional responses may influence their behavior throughout life."

This hot and cool framework may seem discouraging if you are the kind of person that usually falls into the camp of impulsivity and emotion. Whether it's lashing out at your spouse or kids when they do something wrong instead of taking a deep breath or eating an entire bar of chocolate in seconds rather than savoring it slowly. But while the researchers from Stanford may have suggested that this hot and cool framework is a dichotomy—in other words, you're either one or the other and there's not much you can do about it— I'm here to tell you that you can change into the type of person who is able to delay gratification for success. It's all about reframing your mind to focus on the reward system.

Switch off and savor the rewards

We live in a world that's quite different to how it was, even ten years ago. The information age has massively blurred the lines between work, rest, and play, and I believe our quality of life has suffered enormously because of it. We're always switched "on" whether it's checking our email while we watch a TV show, eating lunch at our desk, or taking calls on the weekend. These days it's hard to tell what is work, what is a reward, and what is rest, as they all seem to meld into one.

If you want to become the type of person who is able to delay gratification, then you need to set up a rewards system and a spirit of really savoring the pleasurable things in life. In other words, if you're not naturally inclined to delay gratification, it's not enough to simply try and force it into your life. You need to emphasize the upside that comes from delaying gratification.

This can mean structuring your morning or evening around doing your chores and then rewarding yourself once they're done. And once you reach that reward, you need to slow down and really focus on it. Don't force the bar of chocolate into your mouth while watching TV, eat it mindfully and focus on the flavors. Don't watch your favorite TV show while folding the laundry, sit down under your favorite blanket and really relax. The more you can train yourself to savor even life's simplest pleasures, the more incentivized you will be to delay the gratification that leads to them. Once you do that, you won't even have to think about walking into the house and getting your chores done efficiently before you enjoy a glass of wine; it will just happen naturally.

Learning to really savor your rewards, whether it's something simple like a nice latte or a big dinner out after you've finished a project, can really have an impact on your life. I'm afraid it's such a dwindling skill in our world; there are just too many people who are too impatient to move on to the next bigger and brighter thing. I've worked with so many wealthy clients who have unlimited funds to enjoy all the finer things in life, but they never take the time or attention to truly enjoy those things. Instead, they zoom from one thing to the next, never satisfied to simply stop and smell the proverbial roses. Learning to savor life's small moments as rewards—and put off enjoying them until you've completed a task—doesn't require you to have much money at all. It's all about where you focus your attention.

Indeed, the nice thing about learning to savor rewards is that you can work it into every micro and macro facet of your life, from rewarding yourself during your day with a cup of tea or watching a funny YouTube video after you've completed a task, to booking a holiday once you've finally shipped your big work project for the year. It's a form of life enrichment that is basically free, and it can really enhance your everyday routine.

Success is not just about how much money you earn or accolades you have. After all, those things don't mean much if you never enjoy them. The people who enjoy life the most have learned how to both delay gratification *and* savor the rewards, big and small, when they come.

Delaying gratification and savoring rewards is especially key if, like many of my clients, you are an entrepreneur or freelancer that works for yourself. These types of working environments can be very hard on people's mental health, as the normal trappings of office hours and bosses giving you validation don't exist. As you wait for funding for your startup or wait for a large client to finally pay you for your work, it can feel like you're getting nowhere and achieving nothing. You are, of course, but just on a different timescale and metric system than other people.

If you are this kind of worker, it's key for you to embed rewards you can savor into your work week, especially if you are the type of person who is prone to overwork. You see, for a lot of people, delaying gratification isn't the problem; it's their failure to reap the rewards once they've done the work. This can cause burnout and overwork, which are things I've seen in so many of my clients. While the "overnight success" may be a powerful myth in our culture, most people who undertake high-risk careers know that it is false. What they may not know, however, is that it's vital to reward yourself on the way to becoming successful. You can't just chip away hour after hour without taking time to reward yourself for the hours you are putting in. Rewarding yourself will make you stronger and more able to stick it out until you are an unquestionable success story and leader in your field.

I love this advice from the author and Forbes magazine columnist Michael Simmons, who has studied the science of success: "In a world where everyone is speeding up and cramming their schedule to get ahead, the modern knowledge worker should do the opposite: Slow down, work less, learn more, and think long-term. To get started, follow the 5-hour rule: For an hour a day, invest in compound time: Take that nap, enjoy that walk, read that book, have that conversation. You may doubt yourself, feel guilty or even worry you're "wasting" time... You're not! Step away from your 'to do' list, just for an hour, and invest in your future. This approach has worked for some of the world's greatest minds. It can work for you, too."

Another wonderful effect of learning to delay gratification and then make your phone call, have your screen time, even your latte or dinner a reward to be savoured and appreciated is that you train your mind to get so much pleasure from simple things that when you get big rewards it feels even better and you live in a state of perpetual gratitude. Start telling yourself that your first coffee of the day, the fragrance of your shower gel, slipping into clean sheets and the sound of your children laughing gives you immense pleasure and it will soon become true and will train your mind to experience more pleasure on a daily basis.

Your mind is like a classroom of three-year-olds

Going back to the marshmallow experiment, I want you to think of your mind like a classroom of preschoolers. If you leave it up to them, most of those preschoolers will simply eat the marshmallow right away when offered. Instead, you need to give your mind clear, direct and specific advice about how your day is going to unfold and what rewards you're going to reap for it later on.

If you think about it, parents do this with children all the time. We say "eat your dinner and then you can have your ice cream" or "tidy your room and then you can play video games." We need to employ those same tactics with our mind, emphasizing what we're going to get done as well as what we're going to savor. It's key to frame one as the precursor to the other.

One of the saddest and most recurrent themes I've seen in my therapy practice is wealthy and successful parents who come to me wondering why their children seem so unmotivated and recalcitrant. I've watched so many young twenty-somethings inherit successful family businesses or empires that have been around for decades, which then promptly go under at the hands of the younger generation. While you may assume this is because these children simply don't know how to work hard, it's often deeper than that.

These children are very often angry at their parents for robbing them of one of life's great gifts: the feeling of achievement. You see, this is sad proof that even if you've been given all the rewards—cars, houses, companies, etc— they mean nothing in the absence of hard work. It is in the *earning* that we are able to fully *enjoy* our rewards. Just as you can't teach yourself to delay gratification without focusing on savoring the rewards, you can't truly savor the rewards without the delay and hard work that come before them.

Whether you are the type of person who struggles to delay gratification or the type of person who never slows down enough to reap the rewards, the clear instructions with which you command your mind are key. If you feel you need extra help with this, I invite you to listen to my hypnotic exercise "The Healing Vortex", which provides direct and explicit instructions to your mind to increase your wellness and let go of old issues.

You find the exercise here: www.iamenough.com/resources

CHAPTER SEVEN
Caveman Bodies Living In Modern Times

In a battle between logic and emotion, emotion always wins.
Marisa Peer, Author

Throughout my career, clients have come to me with a shopping list of things they'd like to have fixed. From money to relationships, to mental health, to career, they see their problems as a disparate list of items to tick off, rather than various manifestations of a larger theme they cannot see.

Whenever I hear a client list the reasons they have come to the therapy room, I tell them that we are not going to treat the symptoms of their problems, but the cause. For so many people, one of these symptoms is weight loss, body image, and dieting, which is what this chapter will be devoted to.

You might be thinking: In a book devoted to some of life's most meaningful questions—How can I love myself? How can I find purpose? How can I overcome being a victim of my past? How does someone being ten pounds overweight factor in? I can see where the question comes from. Our culture is obsessed with weight and weight loss almost to the point of satire. It has seeped not only into our healthcare systems and grocery aisles but into our popular culture and TV shows and entertainment, too. However, the vast majority of those examples of weight loss culture are merely treating the symptom of weight loss. My goal is to treat the cause once and for all. It's what I call, "What Lies Beneath", meaning the presenting problem is not the problem; what lies beneath it and causes it is the problem.

In the first few chapters, we focused on patterns of thought. In the last three chapters, I taught you patterns of action. As you may know by now, these patterns can be used in a positive or negative way—but however you use them, they will be immensely powerful. Let's take a look at one of the more common ways that food as a pattern of thought becomes a self-defeating pattern of action.

Somewhere along the way in your life, perhaps you learned that food was scarce. Perhaps it was because, in your family, funds and resources were very limited, and thus food actually wasn't readily available all the time and there was no money for treats or luxury foods. Or, perhaps your parents grew up in a climate of scarcity, so their aversion to wasting food was passed on to you, even though it wasn't economically necessary.

Whatever the reason, you were admonished for wasting food at the dinner table, and you weren't allowed to have the tasty and sugar-filled food and snacks you desired at home, as those were considered a waste of precious funds. Furthermore, perhaps your mom punished you when she found out you'd been buying sweets after school from the shop. This punishment and scarcity caused you pain—you wanted to eat yummy things but you weren't allowed and you got punished for desiring them. You felt embarrassed and full of shame from an early age. Even worse, some parents buy treats only for themselves but don't allow their children to have them. Maybe your parents were fanatical about health and did not allow you to have sugar even though your friends had it. So, you felt deprived and trying to cut out sugar now simply intensifies those feelings of deprivation.

The culture of food, thinness, and dieting that our media promotes further underlines your shame of having to "sneak" the treats and food you loved so you could be "good." Furthermore, you always felt obliged to finish whatever was on your plate, even if you weren't hungry because you associated pain with wasting food. You got yourself into a situation where having what you wanted— treats—was not only forbidden but laden with negative emotions. And leaving food on your plate was simply not an option.

Now you are an adult and your parents or caregivers are no longer around to influence your decisions about food. However, your mind still remembers the pain that's associated with deprivation around your favorite delicious treats. So, each and every time you start a diet, your mind sabotages you with this pattern of thought. It is operating on the outdated information that dieting (or scarcity, to be more specific) causes you pain. Of course, now that you're an adult who can make your own decisions around what to eat, there is no scarcity. What really causes you pain now is your inability to lose weight, but your subconscious mind has not yet been told otherwise. It's operating on outdated information.

So how could you change this pattern of thought? Going back to what we learned in Chapters One and Two, you can communicate with yourself in a detailed, specific way leaving no room for misinterpretation or confusion so that your mind will help you move towards your present-day goals, not your inherited ones. For example, if you've started a new eating plan and are trying to avoid carbohydrates or fried foods, and yet you feel drawn to the pizza shop or the ice cream store, how should you respond?

The old information (or habit of thought) would go like this: "I want that pizza so badly, but I CANNOT have it. I HAVE to resist eating pizza or I will fail at my diet." Your mind sees that as a direct threat to its goal of avoiding scarcity—you're basically reminding your brain that pizza is scarce!—so in response, it drives you to order the pizza and eat all of it in one sitting (habit of action). Remember, your mind wants to avoid the pain of scarcity. However, if you say: "I CAN order a pizza because I'm totally in charge of my decisions around food, but right now, I'm going to have grilled fish and a big salad instead. That pizza will always be there when I want it, but today, I'm making a different, healthier choice. I will be equally full and satisfied." See what happens? Your mind doesn't feel the desire to avoid that scarcity, because you've told your mind there is no scarcity. You choose the alternative with ease (a new pattern of action) because it doesn't cause pain.

If that sounds too good to be true after a lifetime of struggling around food, trust me. I've seen it work time and time again.

We're all just cavemen

You might be wondering how I came to develop my ideas around food, body image, and what drives it. Many years ago, I was a personal trainer in Los Angeles. I regularly taught classes for the legendary Jane Fonda and had first-hand insight into the exercise phenomenon that was so popular in Los Angeles (which has now become worldwide).

In that time, I felt puzzled. I watched people who would work out constantly, with a devotion that seemed near-religious. Yet despite that, they seemed to all constantly be on a diet or fretting about food. There were so many fad diets at the time—cabbage soup diet, grapefruit diet, cottage cheese diet—it was hard to keep track. And I couldn't understand why people who were evidently so incredibly motivated to take care of their bodies were still clearly struggling to feed themselves in a way that didn't cause immense stress and unhappiness. It appeared no matter how hard they tried—and trust me, they tried *very* hard, even doing two workout classes a day—they could never cure their emotional relationship with food.

If that fraught relationship sounds familiar, compare it to that of a baby. In utero, babies have a totally effortless relationship with food. They have access to nourishment 24/7, but they simply take what they need, stop when they've had enough, and don't know any different. Even after they're born, babies still appear to approach eating with a completely carefree mind. Before a baby starts eating solid food, it's very hard to get them to gorge on formula or breast milk; they instinctively know how to self-regulate and thus are totally in tune with their bodies.

So what changes? Put simply, our beliefs about food do. I gave just one rather common example above—about people who learned food was scarce from their parent or caregiver—but in my time working with clients and hearing from readers, I have heard literally thousands of different variations on the theme: "I learned food was fill-in-the-blank, so I lost my ability to self-regulate."

While these beliefs can very often be passed down from your parents or caretakers, our culture certainly doesn't help with this. We are broadcast images of food constantly, often with names such as "fun size," "happy meal," and "celebrations" to make us believe that foods laden with sugar and fat are exactly what we want and need. After all, food companies know that it doesn't much matter what the ingredients are; people will eat something if it tastes good and the picture they create is right. And yet, at the same time, our culture is obsessed with thinness in a way that makes anyone who isn't a size two feel like there is something chronically wrong with them. No wonder we are all so confused about food! We are given conflicting messages of indulgence and deprivation all day long, every day.

You probably already know that what often drives overeating is feelings. But what I learned in those years working in body-obsessed LA was that our environment drives it as well. When our inherited patterns of thought about food meet with a surrounding environment that is at once obsessed with unhealthy food and thinness—an obvious paradox—things really begin to go haywire.

If you want to have a great relationship with food and love your body, it's not about changing what you eat, it's about changing what you think. But, here is the key: You can't just change the dialogue you have with yourself about food, you *also* have to change how you think about the surrounding world we're living in. You have to recognize that it's an evolutionary mismatch. The easiest way to do that is to think of yourself as a caveman living in modern times.

Remember how babies live in perfect alignment with their hunger and desires? Adult humans used to do that, too. When food was scarce and they had to hunt or gather everything they ate, cavemen had to respond to the strong evolutionary impulses we are born with in order to survive. So, if they made a big kill and had a huge source of protein and fat, they ate as much of it as they could while it lasted because they didn't know when they'd find it again. When they found a source of sugar such as honey or ripe fruit, they also would gorge. After all, they didn't have year-round access to unlimited food—and calorie-dense sugar was even scarcer. Their bodies evolved to store up nutrients for a time when the trees would bear no fruit and the animals would be too skinny for them to eat. And guess what? Your body still does that, too. You're living in a time when there is no scarcity of food. Rather, an unimaginable abundance. If a caveman or hunter-gatherer had spent just one day in a modern grocery store, he or she would probably get sick from eating all the nutrient-dense food surrounding them. After all, the calories, fat, and sugar in just one Snickers bar could keep a caveman going for days—imagine what a family-sized packet of Snickers bars could do!

I Am Enough

Your mind and body still think you're a caveman. It does not realize that you are no longer living in a time of nutritional scarcity. So it wants you to gorge on the things that, once upon a time, were incredibly scarce. To make matters worse, those sugary and fatty foods are even more sugary and fatty than the fruit, honey, and meat our ancestors once gorged on when they could find it. In fact, a pizza or ice cream bar is scientifically engineered to be utterly irresistible to your caveman body. *And* it's usually cheaper than vegetables, incentivizing you to eat it even more.

When our ancestors came across ripe bananas they would never think, "Gosh that's a lot of fructose. It will spike my blood sugar and store fat so I will just have a little," they would think, "That fruit will mould soon, I don't know when I will get the opportunity to eat it again, I need to gorge," and gorge they did. The problem is that you may encounter chocolate every day but your mind still sends the same message: 'gorge' because you don't know when you will get that again." It never tells you to gorge on broccoli or lettuce as they were not scarce like sugar was.

So how on earth can we compete? If you've read this book to this point, you might be able to predict that the solution is changing your pattern of thought. While you may still have the evolutionary impulses of a caveman, you fortunately have access to much more accurate information about your surroundings. You can use that information to update how you act. So while your mind may have a belief that if you binge on sugar you're going to survive on the planet, you can also explain to your mind that is no longer true.

Remember, eating is always an act of regression. Whether we are regressing to our caveman survival instincts or we are going back to the baby version of ourselves, where being fed meant being loved and cared for, our relationship with food is deeply embedded. In this way, you need to update what the act of eating represents now. Eating unhealthy sugar foods in the modern world context is going to do the *opposite* of keeping you alive on the planet longer. Gorging on an entire pizza until you feel sick is doing the *opposite* of loving and caring for yourself. You may try to fight this with minimal success but what I have found absolutely works is to talk to your mind in a commanding way by saying: "chocolate has been in my life for X years. It's always going to be available. I desire to become and stay indifferent to it." When you give your mind better detailed instructions I promise you it will respond to them by giving you what you want—not what it thinks you want based on outdated evolutionary needs. It's true that your mind wants you to remember where sugar is, keep you going back for more and gorge on it. What is also true is that you can steer your mind away from this for good, not by changing the behavior but by changing the thinking that controls that behavior.

Once you update your mind from "This food will make me feel good and help me survive" to "I'm choosing not to eat this food because it doesn't really serve me in the present, modern sense anymore," you begin to self-regulate to what your needs are today—not when you were a child or a caveman. It doesn't mean the cookies and ice cream won't taste good anymore, but it does mean that they will seem less alluring, and less integral to your survival.

By doing this, you are acknowledging the things that are driving you to binge on a whole packet of cookies—both your evolutionary impulse and the attitude towards food you developed as a child—and yet you are choosing to serve the modern, present day version of yourself instead. That version will thank you.

So when you're tempted, you might say:

"I'm not seven. I can eat cookies every day for the next 50 years, no one is stopping me or shaming me for eating them, but today I'm choosing something healthier."

Or you might say:

"I'm not living like a caveman. There is no scarcity; cookies will always be there and always be cheap. But today I don't need them."

It's also fascinating to see that in nature we had sweet food such as honey and fatty food such as nuts, seeds, and oily fish but the combination of the two didn't exist apart from in one food—breast milk. Our craving for fatty, sweet food is nothing more than a need to regress back to a time when that fatty sweet combo met all our needs. However, it can't do that anymore and furthermore, you don't want to be a baby; you want to eat delicious, healthy, nutritious food and the way to make that happen is to dialogue with your mind in a productive way. Knowing that your mind does what it thinks you want it to do, the more you can tell it what you truly want (to be slim, fit, healthy and with a lifelong preference for healthy food), the more it can give that to you.

I explained to you earlier that your mind does what it thinks you want. We see this in action when we give in to hunger and eat anything and eat too fast. Not too long ago we died more of hunger than disease and our primitive brain is still wired to be scared of hunger and to make that fear go away fast, it actively encourages us to eat anything available instead of eating selectively. The way to stop this is to acknowledge the scary feeling of hunger whilst telling your mind hunger does not scare you and that you prefer, and are choosing, to wait until you can eat healthier food. Giving your mind better instructions always works.

Four easy food hacks

I really believe in making things as concrete and simple as possible. So now that I've explained the psychology behind why you overeat, I want to give you some easy and straightforward hacks you can employ in your life to keep your mind and habits on track.

As we've learned before, the mind is very simple. It responds to stimuli. So the first thing you can do to make sure you stay on track is to reduce your exposure to tempting stimuli. Put simply, this means:

Don't have treats or temptations in your house.

Remember, you are hard-wired to remember where sugar is— whether it's a mango tree or a packet of Oreos—and go back looking for more of it. Instead of fighting that fact, work with it. Put lots of barriers between you and sugar or other junk food (walking to the shop, spending money, etc) so that you're far less likely to impulsively binge.

If you have children or a family which makes it difficult to entirely eliminate sugar or temptations, then at least put these things out of your line of vision. Put cookies on a top shelf in a container you can't see into. Don't leave candy out on your coffee table. Give the leftover cake slices to your guest. When you do buy treats, buy the varieties you like the least—you'll be less tempted that way.

This hack expands to what you put on your plate, too. If you've cooked a big lunch, make yourself a plate with the food you're going to enjoy, and leave the serving dishes in the kitchen, rather than on the table. After all, if food is in your line of vision, it's very likely that your caveman mind will want you to eat more of it, so remove that option by keeping the food out of your sight. Equally, avoid all-you-can-eat buffets, baking or cooking shows, and restaurants with dessert trays or bottomless bread baskets. Your caveman brain is programed to go wild in these settings, so don't try to fight that. Simply avoid putting yourself in them.

The second hack is to avoid too much variety when it comes to food. The more options you have for what to eat, the more you will eat. Your brain wants you to be as nourished as possible in case there are lean times ahead. But we know there are no lean times. So if you go to a dinner party or picnic where there are seven different main dishes and sides, it's very likely you're going to want to try them all. Instead, stick to a range of flavors and dishes you know you like, but are fairly familiar to your palate. And avoid situations where you will be surrounded by endless amounts of food.

The third hack is to stop using food as a reward. While there is nothing wrong with eating a bit of chocolate every now and then, I want you to know that if you are regularly using food as a reward, it is not in the best interest of your long-term success. Remember, if your body could talk, it would much rather you reward it with healthier alternatives than gorging on junk food. Instead, I want you to give your body better rewards such as going for a walk, buying yourself a small treat such as a new book, or preparing yourself a nice fruit salad or latte. Communicate better with your body so that it knows these things are rewards and not punishment, and over time you'll begin to see them as such.

The last hack is to improve the quality of foods you put in your body. Your mind may think you want junk food and sugar, but let me assure you that your body wants anything but. An easy way to determine if what you're about to eat is something your body wants is what I call the five Rs:

Does the food **roam** or grow on the planet?
Can you **recognize** the ingredients it's composed of?
Could you eat it **raw**?
Does it **rot**?
Can you **recreate** it in your kitchen?

Most processed foods, refined carbohydrates, candy, and treats do not pass the five Rs test. But interestingly, everything our caveman ancestors ate does pass the test. So the best thing you can do for your caveman body is to eat like a caveman, too, with an emphasis on fresh meat or fish, vegetables, fruits, nuts, seeds, and eggs— which are all things that pass the five Rs test.

I'd like to finish this chapter by saying that if you are overweight, you shouldn't feel shame or inadequacy because of it. I have seen firsthand how difficult it is to be a person who is overweight in our culture, and I believe there is too little recognition of the environmental factors which cause people to overeat. We see it as a personal failing, an issue of weak will, when in reality—as I've explained above—it's an issue of an evolutionary mismatch. So if you're struggling with weight be kind to yourself, and know that if you update your belief systems around food, it will be a lot easier to change your habits from there.

The rules of your mind

I am a great believer than we can't fix what we don't understand. I see so many clients who try to battle their minds using sheer force or will to make their mind change, they equally try to punish their bodies and force them to act or look different. They try to force family members and their children to change using cajoling, bribes or punishment with little success and a lot of frustration. You can't fight your wiring but when you understand how and why your mind operates you can then work with it instead of against it to get all the changes you want. As you read through the rules of your mind, you will see how your mind works and how to make it work with you and indeed for you, rather than against you.

- Your every thought and word form a blueprint that your mind and body work to make your reality.

- The strongest force in humans is that we must act in a way that consistently matches our thinking.

- Every thought you think causes a physical reaction and an emotional response within you.

- Imagination is more powerful than knowledge when dealing with your own mind or the mind of others.

- In a battle between emotion and logic, emotion always wins.

- Your mind always does what it thinks you want it to do.

- Your mind works to move you from pain to pleasure.

- Your mind is hardwired to resist what it unfamiliar and to return to what is familiar.

- Your mind responds to the pictures you construct and the words you tell yourself.

- Your mind does not care if what you tell it is good, bad, true, false, healthy unhealthy, or right or wrong, it accepts and acts on your words regardless.

- You make your beliefs then your beliefs make you then the universe makes those beliefs real.

- What you present to your mind, your mind will present back to you.

- When dealing with the subconscious mind, the greater the conscious effort the less the subconscious responds.

- The mind cannot hold conflicting beliefs or thoughts they cancel each other out.

- Your mind can only work in the present tense.

- Your mind does not recognize neutral words like don't, can't, no, not, later. maybe, tomorrow.

- Your mind can only respond to words that make pictures, the more vivid the picture, the more powerful the response.

- Your mind responds better to positive words and to specific detailed dynamic words and instructions.

- The mind learns by repetition.

- What is expected tends to be realized.

- Whatever you focus on, you get more of.

CHAPTER EIGHT
The Biggest Challenge To Enjoying Happiness And Inner Peace

The most important words you will ever hear are the words you say to yourself while the most important opinion is your own.
Marisa Peer, Author

Witnessing the staggering diversity of human experience is one of the most interesting things about being a therapist and speaker. I come into contact with thousands of people throughout my career and I never get tired of hearing about the myriad of backgrounds, life stories, trials and triumphs of my clients, whether they are a baker, a famous movie star or a CEO. As you may have deduced by reading my book so far, I really do believe that the most deeply-held feelings and desires that we all have at our core are very similar no matter what culture we grew up in or hardship we have experienced. This chapter is all about the belief "I am not enough," that in my experience almost always lies beneath the emotional problems, addictions, or mental fixations that clients are faced with. I wholeheartedly believe that this belief is the biggest emotional disease affecting humanity today.

But first, I want to illustrate this with another story from a past client of mine. I was working in Los Angeles on a television show, and as the producers tended to do in those days, they called me and asked me to sort out one of their more difficult cast members. He was being recalcitrant and very rude to the show's staff, cast, and production crew. This was a huge problem as all his unreasonable demands and eccentricities were holding up filming and making people quit. Even I was instructed that, when I drove to his home, I was not allowed to park my rental car—a brand new red Mustang—in his driveway, as he could only tolerate luxury cars such as Ferraris, Porsches, and Jaguars being seen at his address. I could not even park it on the street outside his home—it must be parked around the corner. I turned up, parked my unacceptable car out of sight and knocked on the door of his mansion, ready to get to the bottom of just what was causing him to be so miserable.

As soon as I walked in, I remarked that he had a beautiful home. He quickly said he hated it and was selling it and moving into one of his other homes nearby while he built a bigger one. He then told me I reminded him of his third wife. (He had just broken up with wife number four.) When I replied thank you he said don't thank me, she was such a disappointment to me. When I commented on the BAFTA and award trophies he had lined up on his mantelpiece, he described them as a curse, saying: "Everyone expects you to win more once you have one and it's too much pressure to bear."

I quickly began to see that whatever this man had—fancy cars, luxury homes, accolades, awards, movie star status and relationships with supermodels—it was never enough to satisfy him. He had all the external trappings of success, but none of the happy feelings that he had convinced himself this success would bring him. The more he accumulated, the more baffled he became that he didn't feel happy. He was trying to fill a hole, but it was a hole that couldn't be filled.

I had a feeling I knew what was going on, so I began asking him about his childhood. It turns out he grew up in a trailer park with a mother that often worked night shifts and a father who worked in construction. Each day, he was responsible for heating up his father's dinner before he came home, as his mother was already at work. Money was tight, so there was often not enough food for him to eat the same cuts of meat as his dad. When his dad had leftovers he gave them to the dog, leaving this young boy to assume his father preferred the family pet over him.

"I know what's wrong with you," I said to him, "You don't feel you are enough. And so you've spent an entire life trying to accumulate the types of things that would make you feel enough. You've tried houses, cars, beautiful women, accolades, professional success but it hasn't worked."

Immediately, tears leaked out of his eyes, and I knew I had reached him. This feeling—that you're not enough—is the issue that's at the core of so many people's problems. Often, it's just a matter of peeling back the layers of the onion—whether it's addiction, workaholism, depression, overeating, accumulating stuff

—and locating the point in time where you internalized the belief that you weren't enough. The rest of those issues are just manifestations of that hugely damaging belief.

The source of this client's belief—that his father didn't love him—was similar to what happens to a lot of my clients. This is because children have one job to fulfil in their short time on the planet: to seek and receive the approval and love of their parents. When they don't achieve that, it's so traumatic and disorienting that they can't rationalize it. It's impossible for a child to understand at such a young age that their parent is flawed, that they are loveable *even if* their parent is not able to love them. So, they internalize the belief that if their parent—the one person who is supposed to love them no matter what—doesn't, they must not be loveable at all. They are not enough.

Once you internalize that belief, it's very hard to even know it's affecting you because it's so fundamental and deeply held. Especially when society reinforces it in so many ways, from consumerism to unrealistic beauty standards, to relationship ideals. People develop all kinds of coping mechanisms to deal with this deeply uncomfortable belief, including addiction, compulsion, depression, and anxiety. In my therapist's chair, I've seen them all.

However, I have watched over and over how a simple, profound, and life-changing mantra can replace this ultimate limiting belief and set you free.

That mantra is:

I Am Enough.

The biggest challenge to enjoying happiness and inner peace

I didn't learn the mantra "I Am Enough" in therapy school, textbooks, or scientific research. As I said before, I didn't think it was necessary to spend a lifetime understanding how the human mind works; I was convinced I could find a streamlined way to get to the core of my clients' issues. That is how I uncovered the truth and power of knowing you are enough.

Indeed, I first learned about the pervasive problem of people believing they were not enough with some of my earliest clients. I had clients who were literally eating themselves to death with weight gain. They neither enjoyed nor wanted the food they were eating, but simply couldn't stop themselves from consuming it. A similar case was with shopaholics. They hardly ever wore or used the vast amounts of products they bought, but something was compelling them to continue pulling out their credit cards to buy more. And the same with anorexics—there was no such thing as "skinny enough." I instinctively knew that what was afflicting one, had to also be afflicting the other.

One client struggling with crippling obesity had tried everything—including invasive surgery—to rid him of his compulsion to overeat. But once we located the time in this childhood when he began to believe he wasn't enough—remember as we learned in the last chapter, eating is an act of regression—it was as if something changed overnight. Seeing that he *was* enough all along saved him from the idea that he could "never have enough" food. He no longer had a void he had to fill. Whether it's food, clothes, drugs, alcohol, fame, hoarding or work, it's nearly always the case that someone who "can't get enough" of a substance or habit doesn't feel like they are enough deep down, so they self-medicate.

We see this with celebrities all the time, too. Each time someone immensely talented and successful dies due to addiction or suicide, people often wonder out loud: "But they had everything—money, fame, success—how could they not be happy?" The reason is that money, fame or success aren't enough to counter that feeling that you are not enough. So, these immensely talented celebrities such as Amy Winehouse, Whitney Houston, Heath Ledger, George Michael, Philip Seymour Hoffman and many others, go out in the world and try to remedy that feeling with fame. In fact, the feeling that they are not enough is precisely what drives them to such admirable success.

However, once these people achieve this success, and still don't feel enough, the pain intensifies. Most non-famous people assume they are unhappy because they haven't reached our society's false high standards of what will make them happy. But for the rich and famous who have attained that, they feel as though there is nothing left for them to achieve. Then, somewhat predictably, they experience a massive unraveling and move on to self-destructive behaviors. They give up any sense that they will ever feel enough.

When I realized how universal and widespread this problem was, I also realized how powerful the antidote is. It doesn't matter if you're a millionaire Wall Street banker who is addicted to work and cocaine, or a homeless person who is addicted to whatever booze he can find, the problem at the core is the same. They don't feel enough. But, fortunately, the solution is the same for both, too.

The best proof that knowing you're enough is the answer, is to look, once again, at the behavior of babies. While babies are forming their consciousness and are totally dependent on their parents, they are generally very happy. Provided they haven't experienced a very early trauma, they don't have mental problems, addictions, compulsive behavior, or depression. This is because when you are first born, you are closest to the truth that you are enough. Even if you are born to parents that didn't want you, the universe wanted you—your very existence is proof of that—and that alone is why you are enough.

Then, usually in the first six years or so of life, something tells you that you are not enough. This can be minor, such as a parent demanding perfection from you, or major, such as a parent abandoning or neglecting you. Either way, you internalize the belief and move on. Then, sometime during your life, your belief will be enhanced by society's standards and expectations. Eventually, it will find a way to manifest, in the form of addiction, insecurity, depression or any other behavior you might be struggling with.

The good news is that the belief that you are not enough is not a prison sentence. You can free yourself from it with the simplest, most affirming statement there is: "I am enough."

How to believe that you are enough

As I said above, the common denominator of almost everyone's issues is that, somewhere along the way, they learned that they weren't enough. Not loveable enough, successful enough, talented enough, perfect enough or good enough to be accepted unconditionally. With all my clients, I try to locate how and when they first got that feeling. Unlike most therapists, I don't spend weeks or months of sessions getting there; I find it in the first or second session using hypnosis.

Perhaps you already know what is at the source of your feelings of not being enough. If you do, then read on, as I will explain how you can remedy it. If you do not, I encourage you to take part in my powerful hypnotic exercise which you can find in the full I Am Enough program. This program will enable you to locate the scenes in your early life where you acquired the beliefs that told you that you are not enough. Locating this time in your life can be so empowering and liberating. Many people avoid it their entire lives, effectively ensuring they will have addictions or behavioral problems, and yet they don't need to because the techniques in the I Am Enough program are so powerful in reversing this fundamentally limiting belief. You can find out more here: www.iamenough.com/resources.

Once you have that belief isolated, it's time to get rid of it. Much like earlier chapters of this book have discussed, you can use the power of repetition to do this.

Exercise

Put the phrase "I am enough" in places where you will repeatedly see it day after day. You can write it on your mirror in marker or lipstick, put it on your fridge, put it as a daily reminder on your phone, set it as the screensaver of your laptop, and put it on your car's dashboard. Change all your passwords to contain it so you have to write it and read it every day.

Then, tell yourself out loud that you are enough, regularly. Say it over and over in the shower. Make it a statement of truth. Say it to yourself in moments of anxiety or if you are feeling inadequate. Say it in multiple tenses: "I am enough, I've always been enough, I will always be enough."

The power of I Am Enough is in its simpleness and its absolute truth.

Many people espouse the power of positive affirmation as a means to change your life, and earlier in this book I discussed the power of using specific, relevant, and up-to-date language to reframe how you think about things. But I want to emphasize here that, "I am enough" is not wishful thinking or acting "as if." It is not the same thing as saying: "I am a goddess," "I am rich and powerful" or "I am perfect." Those things may or may not be true and they depend on other people's perceptions of you. On the other hand, "I am enough" is a statement of fact. Every single person on the planet, by virtue of their existence, is enough and is worthy of love. Its strength lies in its simplicity and in the mind's ability to accept it rather than reject it.

While studies show that it takes a minimum of 10 to 21 days to let go of a belief and lock onto a new one, the belief "I am enough" will be easier for your mind to accept if you use the tool of repetition. In effect what happens is that your mind says: "You say this all the time, so it must be true." You make your "enoughness" so familiar to you that it becomes embedded.

Once you have mastered the belief that you are enough and are affirming it in your everyday life, spread it to your family, friends, children, and peers. I absolutely love getting letters from parents saying that teaching their children this truth has helped them overcome bullying and other forms of childhood anxiety. I've seen this tremendously powerful belief work for so many people, and I know it can work for you and those you love. One parent stencilled it onto her child's pillow and onto cushions in the home, another turned it into a piece of art in her child's bedroom and reported astonishing changes in their child's self-esteem super fast. Once you know that you are enough, you won't sit back—on the contrary. You will acquire a drive to build the full and loving life, family, and career that you know is yours for the taking because you will know with unshakable conviction that you deserve it and are worthy of it.

CHAPTER NINE
Criticism Withers; Praise Builds

Belief without talent can take you further than talent without belief but when you have both you are unstoppable.
Marisa Peer, Author

Next time you're in your office or catching up with friends, pay attention to what happens when someone receives a compliment. You don't have to listen long before something akin to the following scenario occurs:

Person giving compliment: "Oh, I love that shirt you are wearing. It really suits you."

Person receiving compliment: "Oh this? I bought it at a charity shop years ago. It's so old!"

Or:

Person giving compliment: "You did a great job in that presentation; I think the boss really liked it."

Person receiving compliment: "Oh no, I really just threw it together at the last minute. I messed up several times throughout, too."

Sound familiar? Of course it does. We are socialized from a relatively young age to demur when we are given compliments. We deflect, minimize and self-deprecate because we've been taught that the worst thing we can be is arrogant. Even if we know or agree with the compliment we are receiving, we don't allow ourselves to take it in—we deflect.

Refusing to accept praise is one thing. But that's not all we are naturally good at as humans. Our other pernicious habit is to be hyper-responsive to criticism. If we write a blog post that elicits 40 positive comments and two negative ones, we will focus on and obsess over the negative comments and view the entire post as a failure. If we host a dinner party for our family, we will allow our mother-in-law's negative criticism to ruin the entire meal, instead of listening to everyone else who insists the meal is delicious.

Why we do this is less important than recognizing the negative effects it has on our self-esteem, productivity, and self-belief. Studies show over and over that giving someone a compliment can change the energy of the entire room in a positive way; our refusal to accept those compliments is to our own detriment. This chapter is devoted to teaching you how to reverse that bad habit.

Praise yourself

The truth is, nothing boosts your self-esteem and builds you up like praise does. Most people think that praise has to come from external forces, but that's where they are wrong. Praising yourself holds tremendous power that the world's most successful people all employ as a tool.

Think of it this way: When someone praises you, they often have an agenda. Even if it's not a malicious agenda, they perhaps are trying to flatter you to be their friend or hoping you will praise their book or blog post if they do so for yours. But when you praise yourself in direct and relevant language, your mind has to believe it. It knows that you are not operating from any sort of agenda that it should be distrustful of. In effect, when you praise yourself, you benefit yourself, too. This goes all the way back to Chapters One and Two, where we learned that the most important words you hear are the ones you say to yourself and believe.

"But Marisa, I don't want to sound arrogant. No one likes a narcissist!" I'm not advocating that you broadcast how wonderful you are on Facebook or tell yourself things that are untrue about your abilities. Praising yourself is simply improving your internal dialogue so you can reap the benefits that receiving praise brings—even if you're the only one giving it. Tell yourself you are warm, caring, kind and a good friend/ daughter/ mother, etc. If you ate only healthy food a few nights in a row, praise yourself internally for that. Or if you've kept up with your blogging habit for an entire week, praise yourself for that. These smaller, incremental amounts of praise have an aggregate effect that can be very powerful on your self-esteem.

Praise yourself for who you are as much as for what you do as it's the fastest way to increase your self-esteem. After all self-esteem literally means what YOU think of YOU, not what other people think of you, or it would be called other esteem or their esteem.

If you're unsure of how to improve this dialogue, here's a good tip. Ask a close friend or family member—perhaps one who also wants to work on their own levels of praise—to give you honest feedback about how they hear you talk about yourself. We tend to have a lot of linguistic habits that our friends pick up on, but we remain unaware of until someone points them out. Maybe you say things such as, "Well, of course, I forgot my keys because I'm always messing up." Or you might say, "True to form, I entirely screwed up the presentation." "No one is going to want a single parent with cellulite." Listen to your friends' feedback about how they hear you speaking about yourself and be prepared to change it if they say you often use harsh or critical words. There is another very good, in fact vital, reason to stop being critical. That reason is that PET and brain mapping studies from UCLA show that a major source of depression is caused by harsh, hurtful, critical words that we say to ourselves on a regular basis. Here is how to stop that. Over the next few days pay attention to the way you talk to yourself, listen to the words you use when you are chastising yourself and then change them to words that have less meaning. If you call yourself a moron or a loser or an idiot just change that to you silly billy.

I was teaching this to a group of bankers and I asked them to tell me the words they most used to berate themselves. One of the women volunteered that she called herself a stupid bitch, while a man said he called himself a waste of space. If you do this stop—stop now—and start to replace that harsh, hurtful, critical voice with kindness. If you would never speak to a friend the way you speak to yourself then stop. You have to be your own best friend and value and praise yourself. In doing that you make it so much easier for others to follow your lead.

Talk to yourself the way you would talk to good a friend. If your friend was late or messed up a presentation, you likely wouldn't say, "You are a rubbish person for being late and you're terrible at your job." You'd simply say, "You did your best under the circumstances and no one is perfect!" The more you can be your own brain's best friend, the more you'll be able to find opportunities to praise yourself when they arise. This is a quiet habit of almost all successful people I work with. When considering your internal dialogue, just remember the mantra:

"Criticism withers, praise builds."

An interesting example from my own life was when I wrote one of my early books. I'm very lucky to have published several best-selling books in my career, but in the early days, I wasn't as confident in my writing ability. Furthermore, from a very young age, when I was doing school reports, I was always eager to get the approval of my father when it came to what I wrote. Of course, he wasn't particularly keen to give it. I worked so hard in those early days, hoping my Dad would read what I had written and be proud. But then I realized waiting for my dad's praise wasn't necessary; I could just begin by praising myself.

Writing a book is a long, solitary process that takes an immense amount of resolve and commitment. I realized in the early days of working on my manuscript that I would never get it done if I waited until the end for external approval—from my father, a publisher, or anyone for that matter. So I decided not to.

As I was writing, I would say in my head that this book was great, would help so many people, and sell lots of copies. I didn't know if it was true or not, but it was that internal encouragement that gave me the commitment and resolve to continue until it was done. When I finally finished, I took the unusual step of sending off the book as an "unsolicited manuscript" to publishers. This essentially means that publishers weren't asking for it, but I sent it anyway. Lo and behold, within a few months I had a book deal and a year later it was on the shelves.

While I was thrilled that my book had a great reception and sold lots of copies, the next thing that happened was really surprising. My Dad called me up and complimented me on my book and writing skills and told me he was immensely proud of me, something he did not do very much and something I had desperately wanted to hear for as long as I can remember! But by the time he finally did, guess what? I didn't need to hear it anymore. I had yearned for my father's approval for so long until I realized I could say to myself the words I wanted him to say to me; it would have the same effect because the mind can't tell the difference. So, I repeated all the words I wanted to hear and it really worked. Once I did that, external praise became less important and I was able to operate like the confident, assured writer I had always wanted to be.

I believe this is one of the *most* misunderstood parts of self-development and therapy. People sit in a therapy chair for years trying to regain the love, approval, or praise they never got from someone they needed. You simply don't need to do this. We all need praise and love, but we don't all need it from one source. While life will certainly be easier initially if you have loving parents, it's not helpful to say that people who didn't get loving parents are out of luck. You can undo years of criticism and lack of love with *self-love* and *self-praise*. I've learned from decades of treating people that the human brain simply doesn't know the difference. The truth is that happy, evolved people who are successful and realize their dreams *aren't* the people who have been loved and praised the most from an early age. Rather, they are the people who learn and master the art of praising themselves. It's not about arrogance or delusion, it's about confidence and most importantly, it's a tool that will help you get wherever it is you want to go. You only need to observe people such as Oprah Winfrey, Tony Robbins and Adele to see that in action.

Once you've mastered the art of praising yourself for things big and small, you'll find it more natural to accept praise from others with both humility and gratitude. When someone gives you a compliment, you won't diminish it or reject it. Rather you'll say, "Thank you so much for noticing, I like this shirt, too. It's my favorite" or, "Thank you, I feel like the presentation went well, too." This, after all, is exactly how children behave. Before they've learned the socially-sanctioned art of depreciation, they are more than happy to accept that they are the prettiest, smartest, and loveliest child in the room. Once you make it a habit to accept praise from all sources—most importantly, from yourself—your self-esteem, brain function, and productivity will thank you. Esteemable people do esteemable things and carry out esteemable acts. The most esteemable act is to be outstanding at praising others and yourself.

Dealing with harsh criticism

Accepting compliments and praising yourself regularly is key, but your work doesn't finish there, of course. You see, the flip side to our human propensity for rejecting praise is that we are more than eager to internalize criticism. Over and over again I've seen this disconnect with my clients: they instinctively deflect praise and always trust that criticism is true no matter where it's coming from. As I said earlier in this chapter, we focus on negative feedback even if it pales in comparison to the amount of positive feedback we get. This tendency is a reflection of the human trait of negativity bias, which is the reason that news channels cover only the horrible atrocities going on in the world. Those things are deemed more newsworthy than the peaceful moments and examples of progress, so we focus only on the negative despite all the good things happening.

No matter what you do, negativity and criticism are probably going to exist in your life. After all, nobody is perfect, and even if you're close to it, there will always be people who disapprove or disagree with what you do or who you are. For some people with overly critical family members, this kind of constant criticism can be extremely harmful and, over time, causes depression and other serious mental health issues. I've seen so many people in my office who are suffering tremendously because they've grown up in an overly critical family which they cannot escape. The answer for those people is that they must learn to not let criticism in and to deflect it with strategies that prevent it from negatively affecting their brain. The rest of this chapter will be devoted to explaining just how to do that.

Almost all of us have met a person who is constantly berating, critiquing, or saying negative things about other people. Many of my former clients have, indeed, been these kinds of people when they first walked into my office. One might assume that overly critical people have everything figured out but, in fact, that

I Am Enough

is not the case at all. Inside, they are usually the unhappiest people.

Overly critical people see life as a seesaw, with themselves sitting on the left side weighing the seesaw down. The only way to elevate themselves or to feel superior is to add weight to the right side, to push it down. So that's what they do in the form of criticism. But here's another truism, as Eleanor Roosevelt once said: "No one can make you feel inferior without your consent." If you don't allow harsh and critical people to pile negativity on top of you—if you reject it outright—they won't be able to weigh you down.

The first thing you need to do to limit the amount of criticism you take in is to simply avoid and eliminate critical people and comments where you can. Don't read negative internet comments and block people on social media who are critical of you and others. If you have old friends who seem to constantly criticize you, simply stop hanging out with them. If the media you consume seems full of critiques of women and minorities and those less fortunate, simply don't read it. This step can have a huge impact on the quality of information you take in over the days, weeks, and months.

Once you've eliminated the easy stuff such as that listed above, it's likely some harsh and critical people will still remain. After all, as much as we'd sometimes like to, we can't eliminate our colleagues or mother-in-law or other critical family members. But what we can control is whether or not we let their words in. Here are my five tactics for dealing with harsh and critical people you can't eliminate from your life:

1. When someone says something mean to you, and it's clear they are trying to elicit a response or make you feel bad, simply say, "Thank you for sharing that." This puts a quash on the conversation, as you are neither counteracting what they said or inviting them to expand further. You can simply say this and then change the subject.

2. If what the person has said is really nasty, consider asking them to repeat it. For example, if a colleague says, "Well, you are so wooden as a speaker it's an insult to wood," you can say:

"I didn't catch what you just said. Can you repeat it?" Chances are, when confronted with needing to repeat their critical words again, the person in question will not.

3. If, after enacting point two, the person does repeat their critique, then ask them the following question: "Are you trying to make me feel bad? Is that why you said that?" Saying this points out to the person that they have said something hurtful and invites them to explain themselves or apologize to you. Often, harsh and critical people don't know the effects their words have, so this points that out without directly accusing them.

4. If the person in question doesn't immediately retract by saying "Oh it's nothing"/ "I didn't mean it"/ "me and my big mouth" or, "No I didn't want you to feel bad. I thought if I pointed it out, you would get help speaking or not volunteer again." If they say, "Yes, I did want you to feel bad," then you simply say, "Well, that's not going to work because I'm not letting that in." Simple as that. Then change the topic.

5. Lastly, if a harsh and critical person just doesn't relent despite all the efforts above, then you should tell them the truth about harsh and critical people. You can say something such as, "Since we are giving feedback here did you know that critical people reserve the worst criticism for themselves? Indeed, criticizing others is an outward expression of inward dissatisfaction. You must not like yourself. I'm so sorry you feel that way."

Indeed, a funny thing happens when you begin to view harsh and critical people through this lens: you may find you have more compassion for them. You will realize that they are not perfect or happy but, rather, the opposite. This is a great thing to teach your children if they are experiencing bullying at school: that a bully is not about what your child has done wrong, but about how the bully feels about his or her own life.

CHAPTER TEN
Sing Your Own Song

But you gotta make your own kind of music, Sing your own special song, Make your own kind of music even if nobody else sings along.
Paloma Faith, Artist

I am an unconventional therapist and plan to always be that way. That is why I created my own therapy known as Rapid Transformational Therapy™ (RTT™). Clients visit me with often very complicated issues but I have found that fixing or removing those issues does not need to be long or complicated at all. Almost all of my clients have unmet needs that originated in their childhood. When they were children their needs for love/ safety/ support/recognition/ praise/ connection/ significance or nurture were not met. Because they were dependent children and could not possibly meet those needs themselves they formed a belief which went something like this: "My needs are not met, I can't do it myself and they will never be met for the rest of my life." This may start as a fleeting thought but it soon becomes a fixed habit of thought and a fixed belief. These children become adults who take that belief with them and because they still feel unable to, and incapable of, meeting their needs they look for someone else to finally turn up to, at last, meet all the unmet needs they have carried into their adult life. They believe that they need and must find someone to make them feel better, someone to love them, someone to give them self-worth, but the truth is there is no one who can meet all our needs, nor can we meet all of someone else's needs. We have to meet our own needs.

So here's a question: What are your unmet needs and who do think is going to come along and meet them? Is it a lover, partner, employer, parent, friend, or having your own child? If you believe that someone else must take on the job of making you better you will always be disappointed and you will always be needy, whereas if you believe you can meet many of your needs yourself, you will do better in life and be a more attractive prospect to others.

Responsibility means an ability to respond. We are all responsible for our happiness; we can't give that job to someone else and after all, if someone else has the power to make you happy then they equally have the power to make you unhappy. Happiness is an inside job. It's also not a destination you arrive at, it's the journey you are on now and every day.

Don't wait for Mr/ Miss right or the right job, home or baby to make you happy—be happy already and you are far more likely to attract more happiness.

If you have a need for praise and recognition, praise and recognize yourself.

If you have a need for love, begin to really and truly love yourself.

If you have need to be celebrated, celebrate yourself.

If you need to feel safe in the world, what can you do to make that happen?

Once you are able to identify your needs as belonging to a small child who had no ability to meet those needs you can also identify that you are no longer that child; you don't need to feel that way anymore; you are free now to take full responsibility for making your life happy and fulfilled.

As a child it's certainly true that not being loved is scary. We feel we will die without love and care and not too long ago we would have died without love and without people. We lived in tribes or walled, enclosed communities. Our safety came from being part of a group whose numbers mattered and being alone was scary and life-threatening. That's why most societies practice exclusion as a very effective punishment. All our behaviors are designed to ensure we survive; we are born with driving needs to find connection and to avoid rejection in order to increase our chance of survival.

These powerful drivers are why children (and adults) suffer so much from bullying and exclusion. These incidents can leave us scarred and damaged as they give us the proof we are not liked, not good enough, not like everyone else. Our need to connect, to belong is primal so we feel we will die if our relationship breaks up, die if we don't eat soon, die if things don't work out, die if we are rejected or humiliated. None of this is true but they are evolutionary beliefs and behaviors wired into us to ensure we didn't take risks, didn't venture to the unfamiliar and thus survived. And here you are, you have survived, you will not die because you don't belong to a group. The rejection we all encounter as we go through life has not killed you.

However, you still feel as if it could and song lyrics certainly encourage this deeply held belief that we are weak and fragile if we are rejected when that is not true. It's true it hurts but it does not have to damage us. Here are just a few lyrics from thousands of songs that give you the same message:

I will die if you leave me
I can't live without you
You are the only one in the world for me
I'll never get over you
My world is empty without you
I can't breathe without you
Everybody hurts
Nothing compares to you
I would rather go blind
Crazy
Cry me a river

It's time to sing a new song with uplifting lyrics. While it's true that it's easy to delude ourselves with tragic lyrics that feed us the lie that we can't live without love, it's also true that survivor songs with survivor lyrics are deeply motivating and uplifting because they do speak the truth. The truth is humans are resilient, able to change and able to cope with adversity because they are survivors. At parties, women will always dance and sing out loud to Gloria Gaynor's song "I Will Survive" or Beyonce's "I'm A Survivor" because the lyrics remind them of their resilience and fighting spirit.

Let's look at it this way. The child with unmet needs is listening to the sad songs on a constant loop feeding themselves lyrics that keep them feeling helpless. The adult prefers to listen to motivating songs that empower them. So when adversity hits you can choose to sing sad or empowering lyrics. You get to choose whether to give yourself powerful or disempowering beliefs and thoughts.

I love the power of songs. I frequently give my clients song lyrics to sing over and over because the repetition wires positive thoughts into them and this is the precursor for positive actions. Politicians and athletes prefer to enter an arena with powerful music playing because it motivates them and also because it puts empowering pictures and words in their mind and the minds of their audience. It's time to pick an uplifting playlist and sing a positive song. Here are some of my favorites:

(I've Had) The Time Of My Life - Bill Medley
Feeling Good - Nina Simone
This Girl Is On Fire - Alicia Keys
Titanium - Sia
The Greatest Love Of All - Whitney Houston
Don't Stop Me Now - Queen
Nature boy - Nat King Cole
Make It Happen - Mariah Carey
Shackles (Praise you) - Mary Mary
Praise You - Fatboy Slim
Itchycoo Park - The Small Faces
Make them your ringtone, ensure this is the song you wake up to and change your thoughts and beliefs for good.

Let's take a look at what I call looping thoughts. These are thoughts that don't serve you, that go round in an endless loop leaving you stuck instead of free and empowered. Looping thoughts go like this:

I can't do this.
I'm not up to the job.
I always end up getting rejected.
Things never work out for me.
Everything always goes wrong.
I don't matter, I don't count.
No matter how hard I try I can't lose weight/ keep a relationship/ make enough money, etc, etc.

I Am Enough

The more you say or think these things the more they become your reality. Please remember every word, every sentence you say is forming the blueprint that your mind and body must work towards until it becomes your reality.

Everything starts with a thought. Your life now is the outcome of the thoughts you think and the beliefs you believe. Trying to change your negative habits and actions only works if you first change your thoughts because your thoughts dictate your actions and your results. Thoughts that are left unchanged can block your actions as we are wired to act in a way that makes our thoughts prove themselves to be true. The strongest force in all of us is that we MUST act in a way that is consistent with how we think and how we define ourselves. The words we think and speak make our mind, body and psyche act in a way that makes those thoughts become our reality. Here's an example of the loop and how that works:

Our *thoughts* control and dictate our feelings.
Our *feelings* control and dictate our actions.
Our *actions* control and dictate our events.
And loop back to prove the original thoughts.

Thought	I am not good enough.
Feeling	Angry/ helpless/ hopeless/ blocked.
Action of thought	I push people away as I don't want them to find out I am inadequate.
Outcome of thought	I feel lonely and unfulfilled.
Re-enforced thought	I am not good enough.

Thought	I can't lose weight. No matter what I do. I'm destined to be fat.
Feeling	I feel helpless, hopeless, ashamed and out of control.
Action of thought	I binge eat to comfort myself.
Outcome of thought	Re-enforced the feeling I have no control over what I eat or what I weigh.
Re-enforced thought	I am destined to be fat forever.

Claire could not leave food. She ate really fast wolfing her food down. She would only buy herself the cheapest food and ate whatever was in front of her. She never registered a feeling of being full and could not stand to deny herself any food. Hence, she could never go on a diet as it sent her into a terrible spiral of feeling denied and increased her desire for food (something that happens frequently with dieting and why they have a huge failure rate). We looked at her past. She was from a big family with not much money and as the youngest, if she did not eat her food quickly her older brothers would grab food from her plate and eat it. She never got the chance for second helpings as they finished before her. She was never allowed to leave or waste food and as there often was just not enough she learned early to eat anything and everything quickly. She didn't ever get to choose what she would be eating and kept this pattern going out of sheer habit and acceptance.

I made her say:

That's not me because I am not five. I don't fight my brother's for food. I can eat slowly and savor every bite.

That's not me because no one takes food from my plate.

That's not me because I can choose to leave food knowing I will always have enough to eat because I am in charge of what and how I eat now and always.

That will never be me, ever again because I have my own money. I choose to buy and eat the food I want.

I made her say this very forcibly several times as she was justifying to me why she was not that child and would never need to act, feel or react like that child ever again.

Looking at any of your behaviors you are unhappy with and recognizing that your negative thoughts and beliefs are almost certainly left over from your unmet needs as a child will end this. Once you have the awareness that the feelings and behaviors you are unhappy with stem from your childhood you're ready to make some powerful changes. I have clients look at scenes from their past and state out loud, "that's not me because," and they state the ending. In doing this they end the looping thoughts and behaviors that stem from the thoughts.

Saying: "It's not me," forcibly and repetitively begins a new thought process. Stating: "It's not me," first interrupts then breaks and then ends forever the old habits of thought and action.

Every habit of action is run by a habit of thought; we first make our thoughts and then our thoughts make us. Then we look for proof that our thoughts are true and this is usually found whether our thoughts are helpful or unhelpful. You can make better and much more beneficial thoughts that help you anytime. Let's start now and do it every day constantly until it ceases being what you do and becomes who you are. Thinking you are loveable while staying at home is not the same. You need the new powerful motivating thoughts to drive you to socialize and radiate how lovable you are, which is so much easier when you know it first. Your body has no choice but to react to the thoughts you think, the words you say and the pictures you construct. You, however, can choose to make those thoughts words and pictures only positive.

To sum up, you have changed the thoughts that you now recognize belong to a child with unmet needs and you have stopped the looping thoughts by stating "it's not me" in a powerful voice. You are now taking the new actions that the new thought requires and you get the new and lasting result. You also sing your powerful song lyrics to wire in the new beliefs because it is such a simple, fun and effective way of doing it.

CHAPTER ELEVEN
Building A Loving Relationship Starts With Yourself

Being in love with yourself is a lifelong romance that never fades, tires or disappoints you.
Marisa Peer, Author

Up until this chapter, this book has been primarily devoted to your relationship with yourself. But so often, the people who sit in my therapy chair are there to address their romantic partnerships and wonder why they can't seem to make it work with someone they love so much.

The paradox of relationships is this: If you date or marry or live with someone who thinks they are unloveable, it is very hard to have a healthy relationship or love them back. Equally, if you think *you* are unloveable, the same is true. This chapter comes towards the end of the book because I want to emphasize that you won't be able to effectively fix your relationships with other people in your

---

Exercise

Go back to the question I asked you earlier: What are your unmet needs and who do you expect to fix them?

Say: That's not me because ......
That's no longer me because ......
That will never be me ever again because ......

Fill in the blanks, repeat it several times and make sure you say it in a forceful way out loud. I want you to imagine I am in the room and you must state it to me and justify it to me.

Your subconscious mind can only focus on the present, whereas your conscious mind can focus on the future. The reason why pain or depression feel as if they will always be there and never leave is because the subconscious mind, which is the feeling mind, only works in the here and now. This is another reason

---

why visualizing changes far ahead don't work because the subconscious mind doesn't see far ahead. It only sees now. Once you have repeatedly presented your, "It's not me because ......," statements to your mind, you can think and believe new thoughts.

New looping thoughts work because you now:

Think new thoughts.
Believe the new thoughts.

These new thoughts drive new actions which equal new results. This, in turn, loops back to proof for you to keep and repeat the new thoughts.

Here's how it works:

I am not a child trying to make an alcoholic father love them. That's not me because ...... I neither want or need the love of someone like that.

It's not me because I see now he didn't not love me; he didn't love himself.

It's not me and will never be me because I am not a helpless, dependent child, I am a gorgeous, loveable adult.

Now we have new embedded thoughts that the mind will not and cannot reject: I know I am loveable (new thought). This drives new actions that help to find love.

life until you improve your relationship with yourself. Much of how to do that is outlined in earlier chapters of this book, but I want to highlight the idea of lovability here.

Bad relationships can take many, many forms but the people who stay in them tend to have something in common. They are afraid to end the relationship—no matter how bad it is—because they are terrified of not being loved outside of it. It is such a tragedy to see someone wasting away in a bad relationship because they feel that no one else would love them if they leave. But the truth is that a feeling of lovability cannot come from another person; it has to come from within.

If the idea of learning to love yourself seems impossible to you, consider the fact that once upon a time, you loved yourself effortlessly. When you were a baby, you clearly communicated your needs (by crying, mostly) and you happily accepted all the love and care that came your way because you instinctively knew you deserved it. As we discussed in Chapter Eight, you simply knew you were enough. It was only when you became older and learned otherwise that you would begin to tolerate being with someone that didn't love you as you deserve to be loved.

So, how does this happen? How did we learn that we weren't loveable? Usually, it comes from comparison, or as I like to call it—being loved with conditions. Our parents might've said to us: "Oh you're so clever for getting those good grades, I love you for it" or, "I love you, you're so handsome/pretty/ helpful." With these subtle statements, we learn that love is contingent—on being clever, or funny, or attractive—and so we stop believing that we can be loved just as we are.   Some of us had parents who threatened to withdraw love if we did not behave in a way that pleased them: "I won't love you if you do that," "You're not loveable when you behave that way," "I will leave if you misbehave."

It's important to remember that our survival as children is linked to our parents liking us and if they appear not to we always believe it is our fault. Our young minds lack logic before the age of three and thus, we believe that if things are not happy at home, we are in the wrong and must change our own behavior, rather than seeing the truth which is the parents are in the wrong and must change their behavior. Small children must idealize adults because they innately know that their survival depends on adults caring for them. Thus, believing everything adults say, they then begin to adapt to try and please them. When they hear these love-is-contingent kind of statements, they go from a state of "I'm loveable," to "Please love me." It's a crucial, if subtle, shift. They then do whatever they can to ensure that their parents continue giving them the love they once effortlessly received. When it does not work they change their thinking to "You don't love me and if you don't love me no-one else will." As clients unravel the long-held beliefs (untruths) that they were not loveable enough because their parents were always at work /Dad left /Mum preferred the new husband /new baby, etc, they realized that they had added on another very unhelpful belief to the already damaging belief of I am not loveable.

The belief they added on was that it will always be like this, it will be like this forever, for the rest of my life. You see the child can't fix it, can't make it better and so they assume it must be their fault. Since they can't fix it they will never be able to fix it and thus begins the damage that can last a lifetime, unless we find someone who can help us change this forever. I think of my role as an RTT therapist as being like a detective and a dentist. The detective part gathers information, looks for clues and works out what went wrong with my client and why. The dentist part extracts all the toxic beliefs and the poisonous old stuff (in the form of habits and behaviors) and leaves the client feeling happy, balanced, adjusted and thriving knowing and resonating that they are indeed loveable, always have been and always will be. It's a huge change and seeing the change in my clients gives me immense joy.

As adults, a stunning number of people go searching for love and acceptance in a mindset of "Please love me," instead of an unshakeable belief of "I'm loveable." While a child might become a perfectionist or a class clown to ensure they stay "clever" or "funny" for their parents, as adults people tend to do whatever possible to get someone to love them—even if it's self-destructive.

Maybe we become co-dependent, or we become a parent-like caretaker to our partner even though they're an adult. Or perhaps we put our own careers and dreams on the back burner because our partner needs to feel more important and won't help us raise children. These adaptations can take so many different forms, but the underlying theme is that we are not good enough to be loved on our own; we must earn it in some way. It also very often ends up with people being in unhappy relationships because they are living to please someone else rather than pleasing themselves.

The number one way to take yourself from "Please love me," back to "I'm loveable," is what we discussed in Chapter Eight: believe that you are enough. If you are in a relationship right now that you're struggling to make work, or you have been searching for love for ages and can't seem to find the right person for you, it is very likely that your belief system around what you deserve could be the issue. Once you take the focus off your relationship with your other half and focus on yourself using the tools in earlier chapters, you might just find that your relationships instantly improve. After all, the people in the happiest relationships are the people who are also happy on their own.

When we are dependent children we must belong, and for so many of us when we are not at all sure that we do belong, that the people raising us love, value and celebrate us just for being ourselves, we only have four ways we can behave in order to reassure ourselves that we matter and are indispensable. The four roles that we will take on as children in order to convince ourselves that we are worthy of love and are significant are:

The Sick
This is so effective at gaining us attention, time and nurturing that most people who take on this role never grow out of it and become life's hypochondriacs. Always at the doctors or sharing their latest allergy or ailment and getting special treatment because of it. The child whose mother had to buy gluten-free foods or rub in eczema cream every night forms a belief: "I wasn't sure you loved me but I can see I matter by the lengths you go to, to keep me well." One of my clients recognized that her sister who was deaf got a lot of attention and was always being taken from Scotland to London to see specialists. She formed a powerful belief 'you need to be sick to be noticed, you only get attention when something is wrong with you' and then her belief became fixed making it harder to unravel and understand it. But once she did she was able overcome both the belief and the behavior of being sick for good.

The Outstanding
The achiever meets their need to be indispensable by becoming outstanding at something. This can be academic or sports related. In tribes, the person who could spear an animal quicker or build a dwelling faster was always indispensable and that's why today children act out these same needs. Unfortunately, the child that

had to get straight 'A' grades to make a parent proud or win at everything just to get their attention grows into an adult who cannot give up this learnt behavior even though it causes them immense stress. A client who was so competitive and always had to be the best came to me with headaches and ulcers and began to see that his absent father only showed an interest when he became a straight A student. Another client said his father paid him no attention until he noticed his talent for sport then he turned up at every game to take pride in his son's achievement. Both these boys learnt the same message 'I matter if I am the best. I get attention if I achieve something and if I stop achieving I won't matter.

The Carer

This child learns to earn love, praise and recognition by taking care of everyone's needs above their own. They will look after their parents, look after other siblings, cook, clean, run errands and do anything to make themselves indispensable to the group. As adults, they frequently become nurses, carers, therapists. They have a belief that love must be earned, chased and worked for and are often attracted to damaged, broken people who they work to repair only to find that person will leave them later. My client was a successful attorney but only dated losers and alcoholics. She recalled her mother being a diplomat's wife and a chronic alcoholic and she paid her daughter no attention except when she had too much to drink. When that happened, she would summon her daughter to her room and persuade her to get rid of the empty bottles and sneak more alcohol up from the kitchen then she would praise her and tell her she was wonderful. She learnt that her need for love and affection was only ever met when she was looking after someone else and of course in dating alcoholics she played out the part where her own need for love and caring was met by caring for someone else. Once this was all unravelled she did a dramatic u-turn and dated someone that that something better to offer her and never looked back.

The Rebel

The rebel is often the youngest child or a child of high achieving parents. Because the other three roles have usually been taken they take the only one left which is to be rebellious, to be difficult, in an effort to get noticed. If that doesn't work they try to take the power away from authority figures and have the authority themselves. Long after they have left home the rebel still acts out a drive to be the center of attention and their inability to move on from feeling unimportant in their childhood causes them tremendous stress and unhappiness. Joey was addicted to extreme sports and was always hurting himself. His wife was furious because they had a small child and was always worried that he would become disabled. He described a childhood where there were three older brothers, very busy parents and the only attention he got was when he fell off his skateboard or fell over the handlebars of his bike and even though his parents told him to stop taking such dangerous risks he loved the attention he got and was the difficult rebellious one that was always in trouble. He was able to see how he carried this forward into his adult life and that it didn't serve him anymore and to the great relief of this wife he stopped taking such risks.

When you understand the role you played or were assigned you can free yourself and take a different part as an adult in a happy, enriching relationship. My favorite expression, which I came to use after seeing this play out is: "We play the only part we have ever known until that part becomes our own." My job is to show you a better, healthier part that you can play. You may have felt you had no choice but to play a certain role as a child but as an adult, you are free now to give up that part and play the part of a loved and loveable adult instead.

What's sex got to do with it?

I'm often shocked by the fact that in my seminars, speaking engagements, and courses I give all over the world, so many people seem to treat sex as some kind of afterthought. Whether it's prudishness, shyness, or unfamiliarity with talking about it, so few people seem to grasp how very important a healthy sex life is—not only for a loving relationship, but for your own personal health and well-being, to feel powerfully bonded to another person, and to have those bonds last, then prioritizing a happy sex life can help make all of these things happen.

Why is sex so powerful? On a biological level, sex changes your brain chemistry and acts as a powerful anti-depressant thanks to the rush of dopamine and oxytocin that orgasm brings. In addition, studies have shown that enjoyable, regular sex is known to build Natural Killer cells that fight all kinds of ailments including cancer. Even when we're way past the age where we can have children, sex also offers an anti-aging effect. Our reptilian brains believe that if we're still having sex, there might be a chance of a baby—so it keeps us younger to look after the baby it believes we are making.

Orgasms improve circulation, provide lymphatic drainage, help your body to detoxify, improve digestion, brain function and mood, prevent disease, help to repair tissues, and keep skin healthy. When we have an orgasm, our bodies release endorphins that flush out cortisol (a hormone that helps your body respond to stress or danger). Orgasms also boost infection-fighting cells by up to 20% and elevate pain thresholds (in order to get your body ready for childbirth). Things such as migraines and allergies decrease in intensity. So many studies show that orgasms keep you younger and healthier. Orgasms also counteract depression, and absorbing sperm has a natural antidepressant effect. N.B. only consider this in a safe long-term relationship. Added to that, we produce oxytocin when we are making love and orgasm. Oxytocin is known as the love and feel-good hormone because it makes us feel good about ourselves and strengthens our bond with our partner. Having sex helps us to feel alive and connected, it has so much to offer us and we should not give up on the myriad of benefits because we get bored or lose our libido.

With all those wonderful health benefits such as feeling young, vibrant, alive and powerfully bonded with our partner—which are totally natural and free—you'd think happy couples would be having sex all the time, wouldn't you? But anyone who has been in a long-term relationship knows that sustaining a robust sex life can become increasingly difficult. However, too many people accept that to be the case and simply give up on sex in exchange for a long-term partnership, and along with it, they give up all those wonderful health benefits I mentioned above. Some studies have shown that 50% of marriages are celibate. This is so sad as good sex is one of the things that can make your relationship special and unique, and it does not have to be this way. A great relationship requires three things: sexual chemistry, best-friend chemistry, and a deep respect for each other. Best-friend chemistry does not mean that you and your partner do everything together, eschewing all other friends, it means that your relationship has more than a powerful sex drive to keep you together. Thus, when illness, pregnancy or sick children take precedence over your sex life, your deep friendship bond allows you to weather that time. Many of my clients tell me that they have wonderful best-friend chemistry yet no sexual chemistry, and simply accept this as something that happens in a long-term relationship. It is true that in the first two years of a relationship we have a powerful sex drive as nature is keen that we reproduce. After that, it turns down in order for us to put the attention on the baby it believes we have made during our sexual peak. Nevertheless, there are ways to maintain a powerful and exciting sex life all your life, once you know how.

Humans have three brain systems for mating and reproducing: sex drive, romantic love, and deep attachment. We need to sustain all three, and being able to understand them helps us. To sustain sex, it's important to make time for it and to realize how important it is to keep your relationship healthy. When we have regular sex, it helps us to connect and bond, and this in turn helps to sustain romantic love. Touching, holding hands, hugging, kissing and embracing all help to maintain attachment.

When I had an agony column in a national newspaper, people wrote in with all kinds of sexual and intimacy problems. The most common were always from women who could not orgasm, men who felt bad because they could not make their partner orgasm, and problems with one partner losing their sex drive. Usually they simply accepted this as they did not know how to overcome it. What love needs to thrive and survive is intimacy, absolute trust, safety, security and certainty. This is what makes going through life with a supportive, long-term partner so great—you know they will be there for you, you trust each other, understand and support each other, and are always there for each other. However, great sex needs something more and quite different to that. Great sex, and particularly erotic sex, needs and requires mystery, drama, thrill, surprise, suspense, the unknown, and even some risk. In fact, our bodies are known to become even more aroused—and our reproductive systems more fertile—when we have sex with someone new and unknown to us. While many women report that they need to feel safe and adored to orgasm, far more report that edginess, drama, suspense, surprise, and riskiness are the elements that bring it on.

When women have sex with someone new, their cervix tilts to attract sperm. When men have sex with a stranger, they can triple their sperm output. This happens because nature is determined to keep the species alive by making us more fertile when we are with a new partner. Nature is not invested in how happy we are, but it is invested in ensuring we are orgasmic because we are here to create the next generation. Orgasms make this more likely to happen. I discovered this when working with infertile couples. I already knew that fantasy has the same effect as being with someone new in that it triples sperm outtake and tilts the cervix boosting conception. I have suggested to many of my clients that they dress up and roleplay by going somewhere different, using visual and auditory props to excite them and boost their ability to conceive. I recommend that men with a low sperm count should use fantasy to increase it. Just going to a hotel can do the trick as we are in a new environment. My clients would come back and report funny stories of how they conceived, but even more interesting was that they almost all said, "Gosh, it was such fun, so exciting, so different. We are committed to keeping this a part of our sex life no matter what as it's so bonding".

When you are trying to conceive it can be very stressful and sex can become a chore. Testosterone levels increase when men feel admired and appreciated. They decrease when couples fight. Women make more cortisol when they are anxious and this can lower fertility. When you praise your partner it lowers their stress hormones and cholesterol while boosting their immune system. It has the same effect on you too, so anything that makes sex fun, compelling or bonding is worth considering. Roleplay and putting the fun back in is easy and we like it. Of course if you don't like it, it's important not to feel coerced into it. One couple I worked with had to have sex almost by rota in line with her cycle and temperature charts, and they were both exhausted. They believed that conceiving their child should be deeply romantic and meaningful, and it all became too time consuming and too much of a chore. I suggested they have sex like lions do, fast and exciting. They tried it out and conceived their own little cub super-fast and loved the memory of how he was made.

What love and intimacy require, and what sex and orgasm require can be contradictory. The two seemingly cancel each other out. Love needs intimacy, whereas good sex needs mystery. Intimacy means being comfortable just as you are. You know you have intimacy when you can finish each other's sentences, when you know your partner's likes and dislikes and can interpret their moods without anything being said. You can share a bathroom and pee while your partner is in the shower. It's wonderful to have this security, but it is not erotic. You may be surprised to know that full nudity is not mysterious. Burlesque dancers, strippers and lap dancers never begin their act fully naked as the suggestion of nudity and partial nudity are far more exciting and erotic. Nude beaches are not erotic as eroticism requires mystery.

When the thrill goes, how do we get it back? People often blush when I say this, but I've seen so many couples reinvigorate their sex lives—and thus their entire relationships—by integrating fantasy in some way. Even if you haven't engaged in explicit fantasy, most couples admit that they often have better sex when they are in a hotel room or on holiday because the newness and novelty of the occasion makes them feel sexier. They have no chores, no kids, no place to be, and all of a sudden they feel like they want to have sex. Fantasy works in the same way, but you don't have to spend money by going on holidays just to have sex!

If you can understand that intimacy is the enemy of eroticism then you can see the problems that emerge in trying to sustain a happy long-term loving relationship that includes great sex. There is more than one answer, however fantasy is the bridge that connects intimacy and eroticism, it's the fastest way to keep your sex life steamy.

People are sometimes resistant to fantasy because they feel silly pretending to be someone else, or feel that they can't measure up to the cheerleader their partner is excited by. They also see fantasy as akin to cheating—as though admitting that they may want to have sex with a fireman or police officer is admitting that they want to have sex with someone who is not their partner. But it doesn't have to be seen that way. Fantasy is inherently exciting, and if you give each other permission to use your imagination and admit you have extra-marital desires (everyone does), it can be a great way to sustain your sex life, together.

The fact of the matter is that people don't often cheat because they are looking for a brand-new person and life; men leaving their wives for a mistress is the exception, not the rule. People cheat because they are looking for a new experience. This does not excuse infidelity but adds weight to the research showing the conflict between sex and love. You can put that new experience into your relationship. If your partner's fantasy is different to yours, you can make a pact to indulge each other's desires and come from a place of respect and lack of judgement.

We are hardwired to like what is familiar, except with sex when familiarity can dull desire simply because when it's all too familiar and too predictable, the excitement and desire diminish. Fantasy can put the excitement and desire back in. Your mind can't tell the difference between real and fantasy and that in itself is exciting. When you use fantasy to orgasm you are teaching your body how to respond, and once your body gets used to a powerful orgasmic response it will maintain it even without the fantasy as muscles have memory.

So many clients ask me, "But how do I fantasize?". If a movie or a story arouses you that's a key to what works for you. We all know the effects of '50 Shades of Grey' which gave people permission to use fantasy to improve their sex drive. Share your fantasy with your partner and allow them to share theirs with you. Take turns trying them out and simply see what feels right and what gets the results you desire.

Your mind is the sexiest organ, and you should use your mind to improve and intensify your orgasms. When the mind says yes to orgasm the body will copy this. The problem is that for so many of us our mind says, No, this is taking too long, this is never going to happen. I'm getting bored now, how come other people are having a response and my body isn't? One of the rules of your mind is that what is expected tends to be realized. Another is that whatever you focus on you get more of. Yet another is that our bodies act in a way that is consistent with and in line with our thinking. You can use your mind to condition your body to be super sensual and highly orgasmic, not just sometimes but all the time by recognizing that your mind is a sexual organ, too.

Talk to your partner about what thrills, excites and arouses you. Take some time to explore what you may like and be sure to listen to what they want, too. We so often go into relationships believing that the other person will meet all our needs, and that the right partner has psychic skills knowing exactly what we want. So many relationships unravel because of this. It's very important to state what you like and dislike early in your relationship. If you pretend it's all perfect and fake your response, it's hard to come back from that later on. It's true that if you meet your partner's needs they will never want to leave you, and likewise if they meet all of your needs. However, it's unlikely that one person can meet all of our needs all of the time. We have to meet some of our needs ourselves, and some we have to decide are not as important as our relationship. Another flaw is believing that it's our partner's job to satisfy us in bed. The truth is, you are responsible for your orgasm. You are responsible for discovering what works for you, and for teaching your body how to respond.

Respect is an important element that makes our relationships work and last. Relationships that shouldn't work yet do will invariably be because the couples have so much respect for each other. Respecting your partner enough means being willing to at least try out their fantasy as long as it's not dangerous. At the same time, you don't have to share all of your fantasies, you can simply play them in your mind whenever it suits you. Remember a few paragraphs ago when I told you all the benefits available to you from orgasms? DIY orgasms also have multiple health benefits and fantasy is a great way to orgasm when it's just you and your body.

It is crucial to remember why you fell in love with your partner and to focus on what you like and appreciate in them, instead of what annoys you. Gratitude is the highest energy to vibrate at, and if you can stop and imagine your life without your partner it helps you to appreciate them rather than be irritated by them. You are not supposed to be with someone like you—that would be so boring—remember to celebrate your differences. We are attracted to what is the opposite of us and it's important in a long-term relationship to remain opposite. One of the reasons men love stockings, heels, lipstick, eyeshadow, long silky hair, and hairless legs is because it is entirely the opposite of them. They also love curves and the waist to hip ratio since it's something they don't have. Women tend to like square jaws, muscly arms and chests, and deep voices as this is something they don't have. Keep these opposites active and obvious in your sex life.

Know that this is not about having a perfect body or looking amazing. In fact, the sexiest organ you have is your brain, and thankfully your brain cannot tell the difference between real and fantasy. If you can combine sexual novelty with your long-term partner, your relationship is much, much more likely to go the distance. People who try to be perfect are the unhappiest and the hardest to live with, and are often left for flawed people. We like warm, real people as the basis of relationships is being able to share vulnerability.

The only person you can change is you, and once you love yourself, you and your partner can have a healthy and exciting sex life. You will have achieved what so few people are able to, and your life will be all the richer for it.

If you want to condition yourself to have powerful orgasms don't wait to be aroused and in the mood and don't wait to be motivated for sex instead accept that having sex makes you motivated in the same way that exercising motivates us to do it more.

You can have powerful orgasms, full body orgasms and massive extended orgasms by telling yourself that you are super responsive to touch. It helps to believe that both your mind and body know what to do. You can dialogue with your mind by telling it that this is right, you are ready and you are super orgasmic, keep repeating this and you may be surprised by how quickly it happens. Orgasms release tension so keep telling yourself that you are super orgasmic, that you have deep powerful rhythmic orgasms, full body orgasms, extended orgasms and multiple orgasms. Women can also have vaginal, clitoral and G-spot orgasms and men can benefit from this too as you can share your partners orgasms and they can share yours whatever your gender or sexual preference.

The more you condition yourself to believe this will happen the more it will happen until it becomes easy and natural and then the easier it is, the more you do it and of course the more you do it, the easier it is. If you have to use fantasy to climax or teach your body how to respond, that is quite normal. After all, when we orgasm it is a tremendous release of tension and in order to achieve that you may have to focus, to train your body to tense and tighten your muscles and then relax them and since muscles have memory this gets easier. As your muscles tighten, tension builds and then releases to a full body orgasm. Keep reminding yourself that sexual response and sexual attraction begins in the mind and you have tremendous power to influence and direct your mind to give you what you want including powerful orgasms. Your mind can make you wonderfully orgasmic and when your mind says yes your body says yes. Orgasms are beautiful and life affirming and nature wants you to have them. we also have an audio recording available at http://www.iamenough.com/resources.

CHAPTER TWELVE
Putting It All Together To Create An Incredible Life

Two most important days in your life: The day you were born and the day you discover why.
Mark Twain, Author

I wrote in the introduction to this book that my goal was to share with you the habits I had observed in my happiest and most successful clients. I hope by now you implicitly realize that when I say, "successful" I do not simply mean rich, famous, and powerful. Success is so much more than that. There are so many people who look outwardly successful but are inwardly impoverished. Indeed, in my thirty years of being a therapist, I've seen that more times than I can count.

Successful, in this context, means something entirely different. It means being your own ally, friend, and cheerleader, even when the world or your social network isn't doing that for you. It means seeing the inherent value in building up those around you because you know how to build up yourself. It means knowing that working towards your dreams and goals becomes a lot easier once you have your brain working for you, not against you. It means letting go of the stories and limiting beliefs you've told yourself or been given by your family and embracing the idea that you and you alone are responsible for the words and pictures in your head. It means being kind to others naturally because you're kind to yourself first.

What tends to happen when a person does all the things described above is that they become successful without even trying. They may not have pursued wealth, love, and fame so much as they did the inner work to address and change how they think. But when you're happy on the inside, good things tend to happen. What I often find is that people who have the outer trappings of success without the internal work are even more unhappy than those who live more modest lives. But those who have both—outer and inner success— are really on top of the world. That's who I want you to be.

This observation from my practice and work is backed up by Tony Robbins (author, entrepreneur, philanthropist and life coach), who often talks about the difference between achievement and fulfillment: "There are two parts to having an extraordinary life. The first part is mastering the science of achievement: How do I take what I envision and make it real? And how do I do it quicker, faster, better, easier? There are a lot of people who are very good at that and they still don't have an extraordinary life. They have a life that you see as extraordinary, but I get the phone call from the multi-billionaire who tells me he is miserable and depressed. The second skill is the art of fulfillment. If you want an extraordinary life you can't just achieve, you've got to be fulfilled."

In other words, success without this fulfillment piece of the puzzle will still leave you unhappy. As discussed earlier, this is why so many of the rich and famous among us become addicted, commit suicide, or lose all their money and squander their talents. They pursue and achieve success, but neglect the work of fulfillment, and the fact that they still feel unhappy kills them, sometimes literally.

You may wonder why it is that so many of us seem to focus on achievement before fulfillment. The answer largely lies in our culture. We are encouraged from a very young age to pursue a rather rigid version of success that is synonymous with money, renown, and prestige. Once we get to the age where we are choosing education, jobs, and careers, we are more than just encouraged to go after the outer trappings of success—but incentivized.

While that's not inherently a bad thing, it can become destructive because it is most often not paired with the kind of inner work that doesn't result in GDP gains for the global economy or boosting our bank account. For the most part, people pursue external achievement because that's what they see and are taught to do; they ignore inner work because there are fewer models of it and instructions for it.

I said earlier in this book that I firmly believe "inner work," including self-love and the belief that "I am enough," is the kind of material that should be taught in schools—right alongside math, economics, and English. I hope one day this will be the case. But until the idea of fulfillment before achievement becomes more mainstream in our society, I fear that most people will pursue external success first, and only reach the fulfillment work far later in life (if ever). It is my sincerest hope that spreading my teachings through books such as this will help popularize that message. If you feel moved to pursue this path of fulfillment after reading this book, and I believe you will, it will lead you to the holy grail of inner work and personal development: your purpose.

Finding your purpose

I work with many coaches and train a lot of therapists, and by and large, the most common thing that individuals come seeking help with from a coach is in finding their purpose or the thing they are meant to spend their time doing. A purpose is different than a job or a career. Sometimes it may earn you money, but other times it does not. A purpose is one thing for everyone though: When you are doing it, you feel complete and total peace in the knowledge that *this* is what you're meant to be doing.

It's true that not everyone in life has the luxury or privilege of finding their purpose. They may be too focused on survival, or they may have the burden of taking care of others. But if you're reading this book, I suspect it is because you know that you have a purpose to find and enact throughout your life, and you're likely lucky enough to be able to do something about it. You do not want to become one of the many people who have this feeling and do not honor it—those people are, after all, the most depressed people in our world.

So, how can a person find this purpose if they're not sure what it's supposed to be? Here is a clue: Your purpose very often has a direct relationship with whatever you loved to do between the ages of about seven and fourteen. Why those ages? Well, at seven, you are old enough to begin to develop your own sense of self. And at fourteen, we begin to internalize the pressures and insecurities of the world around us, and perhaps start moderating our behavior accordingly to "fit in" or "be good." But between those two ages, we find a sweet spot where we were allowing our desires and passions to direct how we spent our time.

Now, you might think: "but at eight years old all I loved doing was twirling and dancing!", or "as a twelve-year-old I spent every spare moment I could in a tree." Of course, those things might not be able to pay your mortgage now. But if dancing, movement, spending time outdoors, or working with animals are things that excited you then, there's every likelihood they will excite you now, too.

As I said above, our culture unfortunately is very fixated on achievement. We don't think it's worth doing something unless we can be *great* at it or unless it can make us wealthy and adored and famous. But that's not what a purpose is. A purpose is not driven by ego, or greed, or competitiveness. It is driven by a desire for meaning and being helpful to others.

This may not be totally apparent at first—you might think: "me going to a dance class in middle age is not going to help anyone"— but I've found that when people honor what they enjoy doing, their paths start to unfold and progress in mysterious ways. Perhaps one dance class will lead to many more, and you start inspiring your friends to join. Perhaps you get good enough that you think it might be a good idea to teach your own class, free of charge, at your local community center. This may not ever allow you to quit your day job—and that's okay!—but the joy you'll feel from living out your purpose in some way will make you view your day job entirely differently: a something that allows you to live your purpose.

From all my work with people, I truly believe that the largest cause of depression is failing to follow your heart's desire in a profound and deep way. Don't allow yourself to do this. Even if it seems impractical, unimpressive, small, or completely random, find a way to follow your curiosity about your calling and I can guarantee that wonderful things will unfold.

And don't forget, whatever form it may take, when you love what you do, you have purpose. And when you share that purpose you have meaning.

Habits of action versus habits of thought

You'll remember earlier on I delineated the difference between habits of thought and habits of action. Most of us have habits of thought, we are just not aware of them. We indulge in critical self-dialogue without realizing that doing so is a choice that has a major impact on how we feel and move through the world. In psychology, these inner forces are often called "saboteurs" and people allow a range of them to affect their lives. Whether it's the inner Judge, the Controller, the Restless, the Stickler, the Pleaser, the Avoider, the Victim, the Hyper-Vigilant, the Hyper-Achiever, or the Hyper-Rational, these saboteurs can run the show if we allow them.

As one researcher from Stanford University found: "Some of the world's most outwardly successful people are ruled by their various saboteurs. Using negative emotions as fuel to push them, they'll ultimately fall short of their true potential." In other words, while the saboteurs may be helpful in getting you outward success and achievement (via things such as making you a perfectionist, workaholic, or cut-throat competitor) they will never make you happy if you allow them to rule your mind.

Much of the material in the previous chapters is designed to help you overcome these saboteurs using one of two methods: habits of thoughts and habits of action. I started the book with habits of thought that you can implement in tiny and large ways throughout your life.

The first habit of thought was learning that your mind does what it thinks you want it to do. As I explained, the mind is always operating in this fashion; most people just aren't aware of it. If every time you drive to the office you think, "This is going to be hell," then your brain takes that cue and makes you feel accordingly. However, if you communicate yourself in a precise, detailed, and specific way, your mind will help you move towards your goals, rather than sabotaging them. Just as we update our software on our phones and laptops, we have to update the way our brain operates.

The next habit of thought was controlling the words and pictures in your head. I explained how babies can't be afraid of flying—even though it's wildly unfamiliar to them—because they haven't learned to associate it with negativity or fear. We were all born with this phenomenal confidence—not just about flying, about everything—but we unlearn it as we grow up. The answer is to lie, cheat, and steal. That is, to lie to your brain, cheat fear, and steal back the confidence you were born with. Even if something fills you with dread or fear, if you replace those images and words with a more neutral one, you can lessen the effect that a given event or occurrence has on you. Remember, a needle is perceived differently by a heroin addict versus a nurse versus someone with a needle phobia. The difference isn't in the needle but in the perception of it. You and you alone have power over this perception—so use it!

The third habit of thought I taught you, in Chapter Three, was making the familiar unfamiliar and the unfamiliar familiar. A frustrating quirk of the brain is that it always craves the familiar, even that which we know isn't helpful to us anymore. It's why diets fail, people choose bad relationship partners, and lottery winners lose their money as fast as they can spend it. But it doesn't have to be that way. If you think consciously about what you'd like to make familiar *and* unfamiliar, you can begin to distance yourself from the bad and move towards the good. If you know the things you tend to move towards and away from, you can begin to intervene before mental habits take over. That's where your real power lies. As I wrote in Chapter Three, if you go to the finish line of a marathon, it's not filled with life-long runners—it's filled with people who made getting up to run familiar, many of whom used to more commonly sit on the couch.

In Chapter Four, we switched to a habit of action, rather than a habit of thought. I told you that successful people learn not only to do what they hate but to do what they hate first to get it out of the way. Note that this doesn't mean learning to love doing what you hate—it would be hard to love doing your taxes, for example—but you can learn to love the feeling of accomplishment that comes after doing what you hate and getting it out of the way. We also explored this through the science behind habit formation, and that the cue, behavior, reward model is a helpful tool you can use for creating new

I Am Enough

habits, and spotting ones you'd like to get rid of. Doing what you hate is not about trudging along in jobs, relationships, or activities you hate, but rather, a way to get through life's more mundane, but necessary, tasks and feel better for it.

Chapter Five explored another habit of action: taking action in the direction of your goals, each and every day. This is less about becoming a workaholic and working seven days a week (that isn't sustainable, anyway), and more about establishing a pattern of working towards success on a daily basis, even if it's just for five or ten minutes. This can take many forms, from meditation to sending out pitches, but the point is to work with the idea that your mind is a goal-seeking missile—it wants something to move towards. As I like to say, "In life, there are no shortcuts, but there are guarantees." If you do one thing each day in the direction of your dream, it's guaranteed you'll get close to it.

Chapter Six gave us another action of habit: delaying gratification. We spoke about the famous Stanford marshmallow experiment, where the children that were able to delay a sweet treat grew up to become more successful and well-adjusted adults. While the children in the experiment may have naturally possessed that trait, you don't have to. If you begin structuring your day and tasks around rewards big and small, you can teach yourself to delay gratification and enjoy its benefits. This can apply to everything from your diet to your biggest goals in life. It also applies to parenting. I shared with you how I have learned from my clients that people who give their children everything rob them of the ability to delay gratification on a long term. These children often end up very unhappy, as they are resentful they never got the chance to feel the kind of accomplishment and satisfaction that goes along with achieving your goals after working hard—which is another form of delayed gratification. Remember, whether it's savoring your favorite coffee after writing a difficult email or not going on holiday until you've finished your book manuscript, it is in the *earning* of something that we feel good, not the mere attainment of it.

In Chapter Seven we talked about how we can apply different habits of thought and action to something that affects so many people: weight loss. We also covered the idea that repairing your relationship with food and your body doesn't just mean changing how you think about yourself, but changing how you think about the environment that we are operating in. Once we remember we are cavemen wandering around a grocery store filled with sugar and fat, we make different choices about what to buy.

In Chapter Eight we explored what I believe is the most important habit of thought you can possibly integrate into your life: the belief that you are enough. Everyone is born into the world knowing that they are enough; the source of that phenomenal confidence that babies possess, which we discussed in Chapter Two. Then, somewhere along the way, people learn that they aren't enough. This can happen in so many ways. Maybe their mother deserts them, leading them to believe they're not loveable. Or maybe they get teased in school, leading them to believe they'll never be liked unless they are thin. The belief of not feeling enough manifests in myriad ways—addiction, workaholism, suicide, mental health problems, etc.—but all those reasons are connected. Not feeling "enough," I believe, is the biggest disease affecting humanity. The good news is you don't have to spend years and years in therapy undoing it. You, and you alone, can convince yourself you are enough with the power of the simple, affirmative phrase:

"I am enough."

The more you say it, the more you believe it, even if at the beginning it feels futile. I've seen it change the lives of so many people, and I know it can change yours, too.

In Chapter Nine we learned one more habit. This one is a combination of both action and thought: to let in praise and reject criticism. As a habit of action, this is rather straightforward. When someone gives you a compliment, don't deflect it, but rather, say thank you and let it in. When someone is out to hurt you through harsh criticism, use the tactics described in the chapter to deflect it (and, most importantly, know that their drive to critique you comes from their own unhappiness). When it comes to the habit of thought—praising yourself—this is something few people know the power of. Praising yourself and telling yourself the things you need to hear in order to feel good is a habit that so many happy people I've worked with share. Learning to make your inner dialogue match how you would speak to a good friend will do wonders for your productivity, confidence, and quality of life. You don't have to wait for others to praise you to feel good about yourself. Praise yourself today and every day.

Finally, in Chapter Ten, we learned how loving oneself is the most vital ingredient to loving another. Often bad relationships are a sign of two people who don't love themselves first. And then, we also learned that once you find that sustaining relationship, committing to an active and fantasy-filled sex life is a vital (and fun) way to maintain it.

You may have noticed that throughout the chapters we reviewed above, there were several recurring themes that apply to each habit of thought or action. These themes are important, as understanding them will fill your toolbox with ways to hold on to these lessons and implement them in your daily life. It's easy to read a book, after all, but changing your habits and thoughts requires a little bit of work.

The first and most important theme you need to remember is the power of repetition. Every single tactic I've outlined in each chapter works only if you repeat it and repeat it often. As I mentioned before, it takes a minimum of ten days and a maximum three weeks to completely let go of an old belief. Crucially, it takes the same amount of time to create a new one.

Often, when people begin to implement the tactics I advise, they come back to me saying, "How do I know if it's working?" or "I tried it a couple times; it didn't work." What these people are missing is that the power of repetition is cumulative. It's not an instant flash of change, but rather, a slow and gradual nudging of our brain to a more positive and productive place. Often, the shift is imperceptible. When trying the tactics outlined in the book, I urge you to have persistence and stick with them for at least three weeks before you judge the effect they are having on you. We repeat negative habits all the time without knowing it; sometimes it takes replacing them with positive habits for them to really stick.

Though I have been a therapist for 30 years, the truth is that a lot of what I teach flies in the face of the conventional wisdom of the field. I don't advise that you spend months and years sitting in a therapy chair, talking about your feelings. On the contrary, I believe in locating the source of my clients' pain quickly, and then helping them re-form their beliefs in a rapid and transformational way using the kinds of tactics and habits outlined in this book. That said, I get many readers who come to me with a lot of emotional pain and hurt that they feel they can't undo themselves. They wonder if, perhaps, they need a longer stint of therapy to get to the bottom of it.

While everyone is different, the truth is simple: You can't undo your past, but what you can do is change your narrative about it. Talking about your past for years in a therapy chair stops being useful if you're not replacing the hurt and pain with a new narrative. While therapy can be helpful in finding that new narrative, it's rarely required to sit in a therapy chair indefinitely to do this. Many of our issues can be complex but the way to overcome them never has to be complex. It can be fast, effective and transformational. That is always my preferred method of therapy. Once you've located the issues that are underpinning your behaviors, it's time to change how you frame or feel about those issues. The only person who can do that is you.

We are here for such a short time, and I truly believe that life is an immense gift. I have watched clients, readers, and followers of mine from all over the world change their lives in an instant. How? Because they changed their thoughts and beliefs. No matter who you are or what you've gone through, you have the power to change your thoughts and beliefs, too.

I truly believe that through your thoughts, actions, and habits you can begin to do so today, and every day.

I can't wait to hear about your transformation.

Thank you for sharing your journey to being enough with me. Your destination is you truly liking and loving who you are, it's a great place to be and it's something you now have the power to create.

Please keep in touch with me, let me know your progress and send your I am enough pictures to:

Instagram – iamenoughbymarisapeer
Twitter - @IAEbymarisapeer

I hope to see you at one of my I am enough seminars soon.

Here's looking at the new 'always enough' you.

With love from

Marisa Peer

BIBLIOGRAPHY

p. 20   Research: Gender Stereotypes About Intellectual Ability Emerge Early and Influence Children's Interests by Lin Bian, Sarah-Jane Leslie, Andrei Cimpian, (Science Vol 355, Issue 6323), 2017

p. 22   What becomes of Lottery Winners, (Atlantic Magazine), 2016

p. 22   What do National Lottery winners spend their money on? Camelot Group and Oxford Economics Group survey

p. 22   Research: The Ticket to Easy Street? The Financial Consequences of Winning the Lottery by Scott Hankins, Mark Hoekstra, Paige Marta Skiba, (Berkeley), 2016

p. 37   Charles Duhigg, The Power of Habit: Why We Do What We Do In Life And Business, (Random House), 2012

p. 46   Deepak Chopra Article: How The Law of Attraction Works, (oprah.com), 2010

p. 49   Delaying Gratification, American Psychological Association

p. 53   Michael Simmons Article: I spent years discovering the simple tactics gurus like Oprah, Einstein, and Buffett used to become successful—here they are, (quartz.com), 2017

p. 86   Five Strategies to Challenge Negative Thoughts, Luke Stangel, (Stanford Business magazine), 2017